Powerful Biblical Preaching

PRACTICAL POINTERS FROM MASTER PREACHERS

DEREK J. MORRIS

POWERFUL BIBLICAL PREACHING
Published by TRILOGY Scripture Resources

www.powerfulbiblicalpreaching.com

ISBN: 978-1-936929-05-4

The author assumes full responsibility for the accuracy of all facts, statistics, and quotations as cited in this book.

Cover Design and Page Composition: Monika Bliss Morris

Printed in the United States of America
First Edition 2005
Revised and Enlarged Second Edition 2012

CONTENTS

ACKNOWLEDGEMENTS

Thanks to all the students in my preaching classes at Southern Adventist University and to all the pastors in my preaching workshops around the world. My interaction with each of you has reinforced the importance of striving for excellence in preaching by the power of the Holy Spirit. Thanks to Dr. Jack Blanco and Dr. Jud Lake for their encouragement and feedback in the preparation of this preaching resource. Thanks to Monika Bliss Morris and Eve Parker who provided invaluable feedback in the shaping and editing of the manuscript. And thanks to my wife Bodil, my most devoted and prayerful preaching coach. May this book bring honor to the One who alone is worthy.

PREFACE

This book represents the distillation of almost two decades of interaction with some of the finest preachers and homileticians in the English-speaking world. The goal of this process was to provide practical pointers for powerful biblical preaching. Whether you are a full-time pastor who preaches every week or a lay preacher preparing your first sermon, this book will provide valuable resources as you strive for excellence in your preaching. At the end of each chapter, you will find reflection/discussion questions. If you are reading this book by yourself, take time at the end of each chapter to read the reflection questions. Apply what you have learned to your own preaching ministry. Ideally, this book should be read with a group of colleagues. Read one chapter per week and meet to review the discussion questions. This small group interaction will help you maximize your learning from each chapter.

It is my earnest prayer that the practical pointers for powerful bibilcal preaching contained in this book will be used by God to bless your life and enhance your preaching ministry. May you be able to say with joy, "The Spirit of the Lord is upon me because He has anointed me to preach" (Luke 4:18).

ONE

PRACTICAL POINTERS FROM
THE PREACHING MINISTRY OF JESUS

"Lord, teach us to preach!"[1] We wish the disciples had made such a request. We could have all benefited from some practical pointers on preaching from the Master Preacher. Yet, as we examine the life and teachings of Jesus, we discover several pointers that can revolutionize our preaching ministry.

Preach in the power of the Holy Spirit

Jesus clearly testified that the Spirit of the Lord had anointed Him to preach (Luke 4:18). Would it be too bold to assert that we have no place preaching the Word of God until we have first been anointed by the Spirit of God? Jesus told His preaching students to wait in Jerusalem until they received the promise of the Father (Acts 1:4, 5, 8). After the heavenly anointing at Pentecost, the followers of Jesus went out to preach in the power of the Holy Spirit.

A case in point is Stephen the deacon, who is described as "full of faith and the Holy Spirit" (Acts 6:5), and also as "full of faith and power" (verse 8). When Stephen preached, his hearers "were not able to resist the wisdom and the Spirit by which he spoke" (verse 10). Even Stephen's nonverbal communication was an irrefutable witness: "And all who sat in the council, looking steadfastly at him, saw his face as the face of an angel" (verse 15). His life demonstrated that when preachers are filled with the Holy Spirit, they are full of power. You will preach with a holy boldness (Acts 4:29-31; 13:6-12).

If we follow the clear teaching of Jesus found in Luke 11:7-13 and John 14:12-18, we too can declare with confidence that "the Spirit of the Lord is upon me because He has anointed me to preach."

Bathe your sermon preparation and delivery in prayer

Jesus, the Master Preacher, devoted large amounts of time to prayer. As He prepared to preach in the synagogues throughout Galilee, Jesus rose early in the morning, departed to a solitary place, and prayed (Mark 1:35-39). Prior to preaching His strategic sermon on the bread of life, Jesus spent hours in prayer (Matt. 14:23-25). For Jesus, preaching and prayer were intricately connected.

The preaching students of Jesus realized that those who minister the Word must also devote themselves to prayer (Acts 6:4). The intense season of prayer by the followers of Jesus prior to Pentecost was not only an essential preparation for the Spirit's anointing; it was also an essential preparation for powerful preaching. The apostle Paul affirmed the importance of prayer in sermon preparation and delivery when he made the special request for intercessory prayer "that utterance may be given to me, that I may open my mouth boldly to make known the mystery of the gospel" (Eph. 6:19). He understood that without prayer he could not "speak boldly, as I ought to speak" (verse 20).

The dearth of powerful biblical preaching among us is directly related to the lack of powerful praying. Peter's denial of Jesus in the high priest's palace courtyard illustrates the troubling truth that we will have no powerful testimony about Jesus to share with others if we have been sleeping when we should have been praying. The lesson is clear. Pray for God's guidance before you begin your sermon preparation. Pray while you prepare your sermon. Pray while you preach. Learn from the example of Jesus that powerful preaching is prayed down, not worked up. Bathe your sermon preparation and delivery in prayer.

Preach the Word of God, instead of human opinions

Jesus proclaimed the Word of God, both in word and in life. He boldly declared that "'the word which you hear is not Mine but the Father's who sent Me'" (John 14:24). And again, as He prayed for His disciples, Jesus testified to His Father, "'I have given them Your Word'" (John 17:14). The preaching students of Jesus understood the importance of sharing God's Word, rather than their own opinions.

The apostles "spoke the word of God with boldness" (Acts 4:31) and "the word of God spread" (Acts 6:7). People need to hear God's Word, not our opinions. What God has to say is more important than what we have to say.

We hear far too many sermons today that give only a nod to the Word of God. These days biblical sermons with contemporary illustrations have become contemporary sermons with occasional biblical illustrations. The result is a lack of power in the pulpit and a lack of transformation in the church. These sermons may be entertaining, they may be interesting, but they will affect no lasting change.

Communicate God's grace

When Jesus preached, He did not simply speak about the grace of God. He actually communicated the grace of God. Luke records that in response to the preaching of Jesus at the synagogue in Nazareth, His hearers "marveled at the gracious words which proceeded out of His mouth" (Luke 4:22). This audience feedback is a testimony not to the finesse of His oral expression, but rather is a response to the essence of His speech. Jesus was "full of grace" (John 1:14), and when He preached, He communicated the grace of God.

One of the most powerful words of grace from the preaching ministry of Jesus is found in a sermon preached at night to an audience of one: "'For God so loved the world that He gave His only begotten Son, that whoever believes in Him should not perish but have everlasting life. For God did not send His Son into the world to condemn the world, but that the world through Him might be saved'" (John 3:16, 17).

The preaching students of Jesus understood that they were sent out to communicate the grace of God. The apostle Peter began his message to the pilgrims of the dispersion with the words "Grace to you" (1 Pet. 1:2). The apostle Paul began his messages on numerous occasions with the words "Grace to you and peace from God our Father and the Lord Jesus Christ" (Eph. 1:2). He reminds us to "let your speech always be with grace" (Col. 4:6), teach and admonish one another "with grace in your hearts" (Col. 3:16), and "impart grace to the hearers" (Eph. 4:29). Every sermon should communicate a clear word of grace. It is the grace of God that brings hope. It is true that every sermon should also contain a clear word of judgment, but even the word of judgment should be communicated with grace in our hearts.

Be aware of your audience

Jesus demonstrated a remarkable awareness of His audience. He understood that effective communication is dialogue, rather than mere monologue. Jesus addressed issues that were on the minds of His hearers (Matt. 24:3; Luke 10:39). He engaged His audience in interaction through the use of questions (Luke 10:36). On at least one occasion, He actually allowed someone's rude interruption to redirect the course of His sermon (Luke 12:13-21).

Jesus was attentive to both the verbal and nonverbal feedback from His listeners. During His sermon at Nazareth, Jesus discerned the nonverbal messages of those present. The body language that accompanied the comment "Is this not Joseph's son?" suggested a resistant spirit and a lack of faith. Responding to this audience feedback, Jesus said, "You will surely say this proverb to Me, 'Physician, heal yourself!'" (Luke 4:23). He then shifted the focus of His sermon from a proclamation of the acceptable year of the Lord to the importance of faith.

The preaching students of Jesus learned the importance of being aware of the audience. Those present on the day of Pentecost entered into dialogue with Peter as he preached in the power of the Holy Spirit. Having boldly proclaimed that "God has made this Jesus, whom you crucified, both Lord and Christ" (Acts 2:36), Peter paused to listen to the feedback of his hearers. Their comment, "What shall we do?" did not mark the end of Peter's sermon. Rather it was an essential part of the sermon. Remember, all effective communication is dialogue.

A preacher cannot be oblivious to feedback from the audience. Peter continued, "'Repent, and let every one of you be baptized in the name of Jesus Christ for the remission of sins; and you shall receive the gift of the Holy Spirit'" (Acts 2:38). And again, Peter showed sensitivity to audience feedback. The final move of his sermon happened in the water, when about 3,000 people were baptized! That baptism was an integral part of the sermon, a visible evidence of a life-changing dialogue with God.

Use a simple, memorable statement

On the day after the miraculous feeding of the five thousand, Jesus preached a powerful sermon. He used a simple, memorable statement to drive home His main idea: "'I am the bread of life'" (John 6:35). We can learn several important lessons from the crafting of this main idea. First, it is a simple, rather than a complex, sentence. Second, it is stated in the positive, rather than the negative.

Unfortunately, we don't have an audio or video recording of this watershed sermon of Jesus, but communicators agree that there are several oral interpretation skills that can be used to emphasize the main idea in a sermon. Jesus may have changed His rate of delivery when He said, "I am the bread of life." He may have added a pause, or thoughtful silence. Doing this highlights the idea as important and provides an opportunity for hearers to reflect upon it. Jesus may also have used a variation of force, or volume, in order to flag this idea, as He did on another occasion (John 7:37).

Use repetition and restatement

Jesus not only crafted a simple, memorable statement in order to drive home His main idea, but He also used repetition for added emphasis. It takes a skilled communicator to state the single dominant thought only once in a sermon and have the hearers recognize it and remember it. In the bread of life sermon, Jesus repeated His main idea at least once (John 6:35, 48). He also restated His main idea by paraphrasing it on several occasions during the sermon, saying, "'I am the bread which came down from heaven'" (verse 41), and "'I am the living bread'" (verse 51). If repetition and restatement were important to Jesus in order to drive home the main idea of His sermon, they are even more important in a day when attentive listening is rapidly becoming a lost art. We must make certain the simple, memorable statement of the sermon is clearly heard.

Find practical illustrations

Jesus was a master illustrator of spiritual truth. He frequently used practical illustrations from everyday life to convey spiritual truth. On one occasion when Jesus was speaking to His disciples, He called a young child to stand in the midst of them. What a brilliant way to focus their attention! Here was a living illustration of the truth Jesus was about to convey. Then Jesus said to the disciples, "'Unless you are converted and become as little children, you will by no means enter the kingdom of heaven'" (Matt. 18:3).

Jesus developed a reputation as a preacher who drew practical illustrations from everyday life. Matthew records that "Jesus spoke to the multitude in parables; and without a parable He did not speak to them" (Matt. 13:34). He spoke about casting nets, sowing seed, and losing sheep. Jesus understood that the best illustrations are found where the speaker's world and the listener's world intersect. When Jesus spoke about crop yield, His agrarian audience did not have to decode His message. They were well acquainted with the problems of troublesome birds, rocks, thistles, and shallow root systems. If Jesus was teaching a class on preaching in the twenty-first century, He would undoubtedly encourage His students to draw practical illustrations from power tools, portfolios, and 20 gig hard drives.

There is no such thing as a good illustration—only a good illustration of something. So we should select practical illustrations from everyday life which reinforce and shed light on the main idea of the sermon. All other anecdotes, as wonderful as they might sound, are simply extraneous noise which can do more harm than good. We are not called to entertain with a smorgasbord of interesting stories. Rather, we are called to proclaim a life-changing Word. A wise preacher will learn from the example of Jesus and use relevant, practical illustrations from everyday life to help accomplish that sacred task.

Call for radical life change

Jesus spoke "as one having authority" (Matt. 7:29). He preached in the power of the Holy Spirit, sharing the Word of God rather than His own opinions, but He also called for radical life change. At the conclusion of His historic Sermon on the Mount, Jesus challenged His hearers to apply the truths they had heard to their own lives. It was a call to action, a call for radical life change. Jesus said, "'Therefore whoever hears these sayings of Mine, and does them, I will liken him to a wise man who built his house on the rock'" (Matt. 7:24). Conversely, "'everyone who hears these sayings of Mine, and does not do them, will be like a foolish man who built his house on the sand'" (Matt. 7:26). Preachers are commissioned not simply to convey information, but to call for obedience and transformation.

While it is certainly true that transformation is God's work, not ours, we are called to join God in His work. When the Word of God has been faithfully proclaimed, a call for radical life change is not only a privilege, it is a responsibility. Peter made no apology when he called for radical life change at the conclusion of his sermon. The call was to repent, be baptized, and be saved from this perverse generation (Acts 2:38-40).

It seems that today some preachers are afraid to call for radical life change. They are afraid to appear arrogant or authoritarian. But truth, by its very nature, is authoritative. Truth inevitably excludes all that is error. A hearing of the truth of God's Word necessitates a response. There is no place for manipulation, coercion, or emotional hype. However, we learn from the example of Jesus that when truth has been proclaimed, it is appropriate to call for radical life change. That call should be simple and clear. The result will be a transforming experience both for us as preachers and for our hearers.

~

CHAPTER 1 — REFLECTION/DISCUSSION QUESTIONS

1. As you review the practical pointers from the preaching ministry of Jesus, what are the areas of strength in your preaching ministry? What are the areas of weakness?

2. What are the indicators that a person is preaching in the power of the Holy Spirit?

3. What are some effective ways to call for life change at the close of a sermon?

Notes:
1. "Lord, teach us to preach!," *Ministry* October 2001. Reprinted by permission.

TWO

DEVELOPING A WORKING METHODOLOGY
12 Steps for Preparing and Delivering Powerful Biblical Sermons

---

Every preacher uses some kind of methodology when preparing a sermon. I heard the story of one pastor who hastily threw his sermon together on his way to church—that was his methodology every week. A regional leader attended his congregation one weekend, listened to his feeble excuse for a sermon, and recommended the pastor move farther away from the church. Obviously his sermon preparation methodology wasn't working.

Another pastor confessed he had never written a sermon. He always borrowed from other preachers. That was his methodology. While reading, contextualizing, and internalizing someone else's excellent sermon may be appropriate at times, each preacher needs to discover and develop a personal working methodology for the preparation and delivery of powerful biblical sermons.

In this chapter, we will consider a 12-step methodology I have followed in my preaching ministry. If you already have a set process for sermon preparation, perhaps you'll find a few insights that will help you move your preaching to the next level of effectiveness. If you're just getting started, I encourage you to give this 12-step process a try. Refine it. Make it your own. One thing is certain: God wants you to be a powerful biblical preacher.

Step #1: Select a preaching passage

I wasted a great deal of time as a young preacher wondering what I should preach about. I even started writing sermon manuscripts without knowing where I was going! It sounds ridiculous, but it wasn't funny at the time. I was stressed out, running around like a chicken with its head cut off. I have since learned the first step in developing a powerful biblical sermon is to select a preaching passage. We are called to be powerful biblical preachers so that preaching passage comes from the Word of God.

Several factors may influence your selection of a preaching passage: personal impact when reading a particular Scripture text, pastoral concern, societal need, and seasonal setting. Each one of these factors will at times influence your selection of your preaching passage. The length of the preaching passage is determined by the amount of time allocated for the sermon and the depth of your exegesis. A sermon on the Gospel of John will inevitably paint a broad picture without focusing on much detail. A sermon on John 3:14-17 will provide more opportunity to examine the text in greater depth. Both options are appropriate at different times and in different settings.

Step #2: Study the preaching passage and gather notes

When studying the passage, it is vital that you consider the context. Take for example John 5:39 – "Search the Scriptures" (KJV). A careless preacher might eisegete the text in order to preach a sermon on the importance of Bible study.[1] However, a careful study of the context will reveal John's intention in recording these words of Jesus. It may be helpful to read the entire Gospel of John, which will confirm your conclusions regarding this specific passage (see John 20:30-31).

Also examine key words in the passage. For example, in Romans 12:2 the apostle Paul encourages believers to "be transformed." The Greek verb is metamorphoō, from which we get the English noun metamorphosis. Use of a concordance like Young's or Strong's will alert you to the fact that this same verb is used in a description of Jesus in Mark 9:2. There Mark tells us Jesus "was transfigured" (Mark 9:2). It's the same verb in Greek—metamorphoō. What are the implications for your interpretation of Romans 12:2? Such careful examination of key words in your preaching passage will provide thoughtful insights for your powerful biblical sermon.

Step #3: Discover the exegetical idea of your preaching passage

This is a crucial step. What is the big idea of your preaching passage? The exegetical idea is comprised of two components: the subject + the complement.

The subject is the complete answer to the question "What is the text talking about?" For example, if you are preaching a sermon on Deuteronomy 31:6, what is the context? Who is speaking? Who are the listeners? We discover from an examination of the context that Moses is exhorting the children of Israel: "Be strong and of good courage, do not fear nor be afraid of them; for the LORD your God, He is the One who goes with you. He will not leave you nor forsake you" (Deut. 31:6). The subject of this passage cannot simply be "courage" or "being strong." Six friends will help us find the subject: What, Why, When, How, Where, Who. Is the passage telling us *when* to be courageous, *where* to be courageous, *how* to be courageous? No. The subject of this short preaching passage is *why* the children of Israel should be strong and courageous.

Next we need to find the complement of this preaching passage. The complement answers the question "What is the text saying about the subject?" Why did Moses encourage the children of Israel to be strong and courageous? "For the LORD your God, He is the One who goes with you; He will not leave you nor forsake you" (Deut. 31:6). Now put subject and complement together. Remember, subject + complement = exegetical idea. *Moses encouraged the children of Israel to be strong and courageous because the LORD was with them and would not forsake them.*

Obviously, the challenge of identifying the exegetical idea of an entire chapter is greater, but the process is the same.[2]

Step #4: Craft your preaching idea

The preaching idea is the simple memorable sentence that you want your hearers to remember from your powerful biblical sermon and apply to their everyday lives. It should be contemporary, personal, concise and memorable. Occasionally, it can be identical to the exegetical idea if the preaching passage is dealing with a universal principle. For example, the exegetical idea of Matthew 7:12 is ***Treat others the way you would like to be treated***. The preaching idea could be the same. The wording is contemporary, personal, concise and memorable. However, consider the exegetical idea from Deuteronomy 31:6. What change needs to be made in order to craft a preaching idea? It needs to become personal. Moses is no longer speaking. You are the appointed spokesperson for God. You are not addressing the children of Israel but your local hearers. Craft your preaching idea with your hearers in mind: *You can be strong and courageous because the LORD is with you.*[3] That single dominant thought is the heart of your message. It needs to be crystal clear in your mind before you continue with your 12-step process of sermon preparation.

Step #5: Determine your purpose

Why are you preaching this sermon? What are you trying to accomplish? In order to answer this question you need not only to exegete your preaching passage but also exegete your audience. Who will listen to your sermon? Are they well acquainted with the Word of God? What are their greatest needs right now? What changes need to occur in their thoughts, feelings, and behaviors?

Is your primary objective to explain a passage of Scripture, to prove its validity, to apply a well-known truth to the lives of your hearers? Occasionally, you will have all three objectives in mind, but frequently your sermon will have one primary objective. For example, if your hearers have never heard of the Bible, your primary objective may be to provide compelling evidence that the Bible is the inspired Word of God. If your audience is a group of young Christians, your primary objective may be to encourage them to read the Bible daily and apply the truths to their lives since they already believe in the Bible as the inspired Word of God.

Knowing your purpose is crucially important when coming to step #7 and step #9.

Step #6: Select your sermon form

As I conduct preaching workshops around the world, many preachers, both young and old, have questions about sermon forms. Using the same sermon form each week is boring and may also be inappropriate for the preaching passage you have selected.

Read Romans 12:2. What is the natural division of that text? Not this, but this. Do not be conformed, but be transformed. To use three points and a poem for this preaching passage makes no sense at all. There are two moves: not this, but this.

What about 1 John 1:9? Here we see an idea explained. What happens when we confess our sins to God? Search for a plural noun that will be appropriate based on the context. Is the passage speaking about problems? Challenges? Concerns?

Consider the passage: "If we confess our sins, He is faithful and just to forgive us our sins and to cleanse us from all unrighteousness" (1 John 1:9). What plural noun works for you? Results? Blessings? I prefer the plural noun "blessings." What blessings come when we confess our sins to God? The first blessing is forgiveness. The second blessing is cleansing. Don't add a third or fourth blessing or a few thoughts about faithful stewardship. The form of the sermon is clear—an idea explained with two main moves.

A popular sermon form in the 21st century is narrative. People enjoy listening to stories. But even a story needs structure. What should be included in the story? What should be omitted? Take for example the story of David and Goliath in 1 Samuel 17. You have the preparation, the confrontation, and the celebration. Like three acts in a play, your story has form. Don't spend 80% of your sermon talking about the preparation. You'll lose impact. Think about your sermon form. You can share the narrative in the third-person where you retell the story, or in the first-person where you relive the story.[4]

Consider Romans 6:23. The preaching passage presents a problem and a solution—two main moves. To add a third move is confusing. You may add sub-moves under the problem. For example, you might speak about the problem of sin in our world and also focus in on the problem of sin in our own lives.

Once you have a powerful preaching idea, a definite purpose in mind, and a clear sermon form, you are well on your way in the development of a powerful biblical sermon.[5]

Step #7: Gather supporting materials

Some aspiring preachers make the mistake of gathering illustrations before moving through steps #1-#6. Premature selection of illustrations can be a serious distraction in the sermon preparation process. You might end up looking for a text to introduce your illustrations instead of finding illustrations that shed light on the single powerful idea of your preaching passage. Remember, there is no such thing as a good illustration—only a good illustration of something. So have your preaching idea clearly in mind as you begin to select supporting materials like facts, quotations, and illustrations.

Jesus always used illustrations when sharing the truth of God with others.[6] When sharing a story, make sure it is true and accurate or inform your hearers that this is a fictitious account. Only use illustrations that shed light on your preaching idea—anything else, however interesting, is a distraction. Use quotations sparingly, only when they come with a level of authority that adds strength to your message, or if they reinforce your preaching idea in a compelling and memorable way.

Step #8: Develop your introduction

As a young preacher, I often began my sermon preparation with step #8. That was a big mistake. I had no clear idea in mind (step #4), wasn't sure what I was trying to accomplish in the sermon (step #5), and had no idea about the basic structure of the message (step #6). However, if you follow this working methodology, by the time you get to step #8 you have a clear idea of what needs to be accomplished. Your introduction will:

›› capture the attention of your hearers

›› connect with a felt need in your hearers

›› introduce the body of the sermon

Your introduction is crucially important. It must be powerful and intentional. You only have a few seconds to connect with your hearers. If you lose them here, you may never get them back.

Sometimes students ask, "How long should I take with the introduction?" As long as it takes to accomplish those three tasks. When using inductive methodology, you will simply introduce the subject of your message. For example, you might begin by telling a story about losing a loved one, note that we are all impacted by death, and conclude by asking a question: "Have you ever wondered what happens when we die?" When using deductive methodology, you will introduce your preaching idea in your introduction. For example, having captured attention with a story about someone in bondage to sin, and noting that we all have areas of bondage in our lives, you might conclude your introduction by stating "we will discover in our study today that *Jesus can set you free*."

Step #9: Craft your conclusion

In your conclusion, you have several important objectives:

›› summarize

›› apply

›› appeal

Taking time with step #5 will help you craft your conclusion. What are you trying to accomplish? What changes in thoughts, feelings, or behaviors would you like to see in your hearers? Your appeal should be clear, concise, and specific. Perhaps you have heard a preacher conclude with these words: "May God help us to apply this message to our own lives." I have no doubt God wants His Word to have a life-changing impact in the lives of our hearers, but I am also convinced God wants you to encourage and exhort your hearers to act upon the truth they have heard. When the people on the day of Pentecost came under the conviction of the Holy Spirit, they asked Peter and the other apostles, "Men and brethren, what shall we do?" (Acts 2:37). Peter didn't respond with vague generalities about God helping them apply the message to their own lives. Peter was clear, concise, and specific: "Repent, and let everyone one of you be baptized in the name of Jesus Christ for the remission of sins" (Acts 2:38).

Step #10: Birth your manuscript

At this point in your sermon preparation process, you are more than ready to give birth to your sermon manuscript. Your sermon form is clear, you have a single powerful preaching idea, relevant supporting materials, and a compelling introduction and conclusion in mind. As you birth your manuscript, remember to write in an oral style. This is not an article or a dissertation. You are capturing an oral discourse with your future audience. Keep your hearers in mind as you select words and phrases. Remember you will need to repeat your preaching idea numerous times. You can also use restatement to reinforce that single dominant thought.[7]

Don't try to write a perfect first draft. This manuscript is not your final product. The words on your paper are only 7% of the communication process. The way you say those words (oral interpretation) is 38%, and your body language (including eye contact and facial expression) is 55%. If you stop here in the sermon preparation process, you will not realize your full potential as a powerful biblical preacher, but birthing the manuscript is an essential preparation for step #11.

Step #11: Internalize the sermon

Walk through the sermon like a tour guide. Remember the main moves of your sermon, making sure you clearly emphasize your preaching idea. The goal is internalization, not memorization. Take note of lessons learned during your walk-through and edit your sermon manuscript. Think about *how* you will express your words, and not just *what* you will say. Walk through your sermon at least five times prior to preaching your sermon in public. During your walk-throughs, think of gestures and visual aids that will help you drive home your main idea.

Do a 60-second walk-through right before you preach. What is important here? The preaching idea, the main moves of your sermon, your appeal, and finally your opening sentence. You want to stand up with a clear starting point as you begin one more walk-through of your internalized message.

Step #12: Listen while you preach

Freedom from your manuscript will enable you to listen more attentively while you preach. First, listen to God. Recognize the Holy Spirit's presence while you preach. Perhaps He will bring new insights to your mind regarding the preaching passage or new applications. Second, listen to your hearers. They will communicate with you, both verbally and non-verbally. Effective eye contact is essential. Don't glance aimlessly around the room as if you're looking for a lost butterfly. Look at people long enough to establish a meaningful connection. Be inclusive. Make it clear by your body language that each listener is important. You have discovered a powerful word of truth and you want each one of your hearers to receive your preaching idea and be eternally blessed.

God wants you to be a powerful biblical preacher. He wants to anoint you by His Spirit to preach the Word with power. That won't happen by accident. You must choose to cooperate with God in a process where His Word first changes your own life and then flows through you to change the lives of those around you.

~

CHAPTER 2 — REFLECTION/DISCUSSION QUESTIONS

1. Share a time when you tried to write a sermon without knowing where to start.

2. What is your usual methodology when preparing a sermon?

3. What is the most helpful lesson you have learned from this chapter?

Notes:

1. Eisegesis is the process of reading something into the text that you want it to say rather than doing exegesis where you allow the text to speak.

2. See Chapter 8 for more on this important process of discovering the exegetical idea of the text.

3. See Chapter 8 for more examples of preaching ideas.

4. See Chapter 19 for more information about first-person narrative preaching.

5. Other sermon forms include thesis/antithesis/synthesis, and proposition proved.

6. Matt. 13:34.

7. See Chapter 1.

THREE
CALLED TO PREACH

Both E. E. Cleveland and Benjamin Reaves have been recognized as outstanding Christian preachers of the twentieth century. In this interview they reflect on their call to preach.

DEREK MORRIS (DM): It's a privilege to speak with two outstanding preachers about the sacred work of preaching.[1] How does a person know if he or she is called to preach?

E. E. CLEVELAND (EC): One knows if they are called to a preaching ministry when the necessity of preaching the gospel eclipses and excludes all competing professions.

DM: You began your preaching ministry as a boy in Chattanooga, Tennessee. Did you ever consider any other professions besides being a preacher of the gospel?

EC: No! I was a child with a one-track mind. I have never wanted to do anything else or be anything else. When I was a boy, my father would take me to different churches—Baptist, Methodist, Congregational. Over the past sixty years I have preached the gospel on every continent except Antarctica. It's too cold there for my Alabama blood!

DM: Why is preaching so important to you?

EC: Preaching is the supreme unction function of the Holy Spirit. It is by the foolishness of preaching that people are persuaded to enter the kingdom of God. Preaching is God's primary means for saving men and women. In order for preaching to be effective, it must be Holy Spirit actuated. The Word of God must be interpreted to the mind and through the mind of the preacher. A human being so ordered by the Divine calling is a power to be reckoned with.

DM: You have mentored many young preachers through the years. One of those outstanding young preachers was Benjamin Reaves. Dr. Reaves, you actually began your preaching ministry working with E. E. Cleveland. How have you developed your potential as a preacher?

BENJAMIN REAVES (BR): Since my early years, I have been a voracious reader. That put me in touch with a feel for language, rhythm, and sound. As I'm writing my sermon manuscript, I'm listening. H. Grady Davis talks about writing for the ear. Words need to be spoken in a way that addresses the ear. I love a well-turned phrase. Those words will come back to people over the years. Having a feel for language, rhythm, and sound has been a tremendous asset.

DM: What kind of books helped you to develop a feel for language, rhythm, and sound?

BR: I read everything! As a child, I read Zane Grey. Anything written by good writers.

DM: Fred Craddock would affirm the value of reading good writing. Poetry. Historical fiction. Anything that is written well.

BR: Then, if you write something that's awkward, that's not falling right on the ear, it jumps out at you. It doesn't sound right. You have developed a feel for language, rhythm, and sound.

DM: How do you begin the process of developing a biblical sermon?

BR: It starts with an idea that drives me to a text or with a text that drives me to an idea. Either way, I end up with a text. As Henry Mitchell put it, "If you ain't got a text, you ain't preaching!" My authority as a preacher is not just linked to Scripture. It is chained to Scripture. I'm a disciple of H. Grady Davis, so my first question is, "What is the text saying?" That's ground zero for me. I'm not in the sermon yet. I'm working with the passage. What is the passage talking about? What is it saying about it? I look at various versions. I look at exegetical commentaries. Once I get past that study of the text, I may have an outline that is going to shape the sermon. At least, I have a clear understanding of what the passage is saying.

I need to settle what the text is saying before I go to the next question—"What do I want to say about it?" Someone might say, "That's already settled! You need to tell people what the text is saying." But I may want to focus on a small subportion of the text. Now I'm asking myself the structural questions "What do I want to say?" and "What do I want to say about it?" I'm going to come out of the process with some kind of structure. I need that skeleton. Otherwise, a lot of time is wasted gathering material that may not be used.

After that initial period of study, I need to back off and let the subconscious deal with that material. That can happen while I'm visiting, while I'm driving, doing anything actually.

Then the task is to put meat on the bones. Generally, that's when I begin to write. Writing helps me eliminate what is not absolutely necessary for the preaching of this sermon. I need to begin some element of writing by Wednesday at the latest. I know I will add to that, but getting started with the writing process helps me clarify what I am saying and what I am saying about it. Because of my initial study, I know where I'm headed. My subconscious says, "Now I can help you." Things begin to come to mind. Insights begin to open up.

As you walk through your sermon, you need to have a sense of time. It irritates me when someone says, "Well, I won't have time to finish this!" What do you mean? What were you doing? I get bothered when I see filler, treading water. You need a sense of time.

The final step of preparation is to let the sermon speak to you. Sometimes, this final step reveals that something is missing. There is a link missing for the hearer. Or something needs to be eliminated. That awareness comes after the mechanical part of writing the sermon manuscript is over. It's in that final step of letting the sermon speak to you that the passion is reignited. That's where the fire comes.

Then, when you preach, be open to the fact that there might be a shift in the congregational dynamic. You might find yourself elaborating on a point that was not part of the original plan.

DM: What about making an appeal at the end of the sermon?

EC: I always make an appeal when I preach. Jesus told His disciples, "I will make you fishers of men." The hook and the bait you throw into the water are designed to catch the fish. Persuading people is the principal object of preaching. So it's important to make an appeal, to give an invitation. Let me share with you an incident that confirmed in my own mind that the object of preaching is decision getting. One Sunday evening I was preaching in Chicago. I had preached a tough sermon, and I couldn't see how anyone would respond. I even discouraged myself. So I ended the sermon and sat down without making an appeal. During the closing song, a man came charging down to the front. He responded to an appeal without me even making one! I resolved that day that I would never again preach a sermon without making an invitation.

DM: How do you craft that invitation?

EC: I tell people that God is willing, God is able, and God is available. That's the structure of the invitation. God is willing—I preach the Cross. That expresses God's willingness to save us. God is able—I talk about the thief on the cross, and how the Lord saved him! If the Lord can save a thief on a cross, He can save anybody! And then I tell people that God is available and He wants you to come to Him now!

DM: It has been said that demons tremble when preachers boldly declare the Word of God in the power of the Holy Spirit. The forces of darkness don't like to see individuals take their stand for Jesus. What are some spiritual battles you have experienced in your preaching ministry?

EC: I remember one time I was preaching in St. Petersburg, Florida. One of our church members in that area had married a killer, a very mean man. She had dropped out of church but started attending the meetings I was conducting. One Friday night she came to me with tears streaming down her face. She said, "My husband told me that if I get baptized, he is going to kill me and he is going to kill the person who baptizes me. What should I do?" I said to her, "He can't kill me, and he won't kill you." The next weekend she was sitting in church, ready to be baptized. As I was preaching, I could see out the front doors of the church. A red Chrysler pulled up, and that lady's husband was in the car. I found out later there was a loaded gun on the seat beside him. I knew what he had come for, but I just kept on preaching. Suddenly, I heard sirens wailing, and an ambulance pulled up next to his car. They pulled that man out of the car. He was dead on arrival at the hospital. The man who planned to assassinate me ended up losing his own life.

On another occasion, I was preaching in North Carolina, and a man came to the meeting and sat down. He had a gun in his pocket with his finger on the trigger. Four times during the sermon, the gunman moved forward and then moved backwards. Finally, he turned to the man next to him and said, "Every time I try to get up to kill that man, a sheet of flames separates us." Then the gunman got up and half-walked, half-ran out of that place!

DM: How did you find out about that story?

EC: I baptized the man sitting next to the gunman, and he shared his testimony of what he had seen that day! It was spiritual warfare, but the protection of the Almighty was over me!

DM: Preachers need spiritual protection when proclaiming the Word of God!

BR: A preacher also needs to remember that success can hurt you. Success can put a monkey on your back. If you lose a sense of what preaching is all about, if you start thinking that preaching is all about you, then you're on the treadmill. You are into the performance trap. Early in your preaching ministry, you can be deluded by your church members into thinking you're the greatest thing since Swiss cheese! Later in your preaching ministry, you begin to delude yourself. You love the invitations you get, and you begin to delude yourself. Either way, the delusion is still the same. It can be just as hurtful. You need to remember it's not about you.

I remember one time I spoke and someone handed me a note which said, "Your reputation for excellence is well deserved." I enjoyed that note too much. I lost sight of what really mattered. I let that little note monkey with my thinking. I don't want to live like that. That's what will send you galloping off in panic. No matter how successful a preacher you are, there will be other days. Unless you remember it's not about you, you won't be able to handle those other days.

You also need to remember that your life needs to back up your preaching and your preaching needs to grow out of your life. I know there are people who can live any kind of way and still be very impressive communicators. But I'm of the opinion that the power of the anointing will not be there if your life does not back up your preaching.

And then, just be yourself! Don't buy the lie that you have to go with "the flavor of the month." Some preachers watch the living technicolored televangelists and are tempted to think they have to reproduce that in their churches. You need to be yourself. Be who you are and let God use you. At the same time, you need to work at preaching well. Being who you are is not like rolling off a log. You need to work at it! That's a lifelong commitment. If you are going to be the best of who you are as a preacher, it's a work of a lifetime.

~

CHAPTER 3 — REFLECTION/DISCUSSION QUESTIONS

1. When did you first sense the call to preach?

2. What are some ways you have developed your preaching skills?

3. When were you most aware of God's enabling presence in your preaching?

Notes:
1. "Called to Preach." An interview with E. E. Cleveland and Benjamin Reaves, *Ministry* December 2006.
   Reprinted by permission.

FOUR
PREACHING OUT OF THE OVERFLOW

In June 2003, Rear Admiral Barry C. Black, Ph.D., D. Min., (Ret.) was elected the 62nd chaplain of the United States Senate. Prior to this appointment, Chaplain Black served in the United States Navy for over 27 years, ending his distinguished career as the Chief of Navy Chaplains.

DEREK MORRIS (DM): Chaplain Black, as you think back over your life, what are some of the influences God has used to form you spiritually?[1]

BARRY BLACK (BB): One is my humble beginnings. I believe that growing up in the inner city, in the toxic environment of the public housing units where I lived on welfare, created in me an ability to relate to people across the socioeconomic spectrum. God seems to have blessed me with an ability to connect with people who may not have a lot of education, who may not have many material things. They seem to connect with me, and they are encouraged by my story. I've had single mothers say that the knowledge of my background and my roots has been an encouragement to them, and they are more determined to bless their children by investing in Christian education and by insisting on Bible study.

A second influence that God used to form me spiritually was my mother. She was a saint! She had a love for God and a love for His Word. She had a vibrant, robust spirituality, which she transmitted to me. She told me I was special. She informed me I was set apart, and she spoke with such power and such sincerity that

I never doubted my call to ministry.

Third, Christian schools, from grade one through the seminary, had a tremendous impact in forming me spiritually. I don't think anything was more important than being exposed to biblical principles every day in almost every course. I was mentored by dedicated teachers who also seemed to sense that God had His hand on my life. I was in the world but not of the world. Christian schools provided me with a "cocoon" that enabled me to grow wings and to fly.

And finally, I was blessed to grow up in a very large church—Berea Temple Seventh-day Adventist Church, in Baltimore, Maryland. Berea was a congregation of probably close to 1,000 members. The most gifted preachers were usually selected to pastor there, so I had an incredible opportunity to be exposed to some of the best preachers God ever produced.

I think that a great deal of preaching is taught, but there is also a lot of preaching that is caught. When exposed to powerful, lyrical preaching early, there is an accent you pick up that stays with you throughout your life and stamps your ministry. It's not something you'll get in a classroom. It's not something you'll get in a book. Very often, even now, I hear echos of my pastors while I'm preaching, and I smile. I say, "That's Elder Leon Cox. He would have said it just like that!" Or "That's Elder J. C. Smith. That's how he'd have phrased it."

That is a marvelous legacy, a wonderful gift to have! This reservoir of material to draw from—exegetical material, illustrations—they pop into my head while I'm preaching because of this rich heritage. I was a member of a great church for most of my childhood, and each time the door of the church opened, my mother had us there. Early morning prayer service. Wednesday night prayer meeting. Sunday night evangelistic meeting. Sabbath, we stayed for the whole day! I didn't always think it was wonderful, but it certainly provided me with a wonderful heritage.

DM: So there was your mother and also some of the pastors from your church. Who are some other significant mentors in terms of your preaching?

BB: I was exposed fairly early to taped sermons and sermons on records. I must have been seven or eight years of age when I first heard a sermon by Peter Marshall entitled "Were You There?" I just could not believe the lyrical beauty of what I was listening to. He was describing the morning sun coming up over the city of David.

I sensed something of the music of preaching and something of the possibilities of preaching.

My horizons were stretched. Preaching is not simply lining up Bible verses and proof texting. Preaching is more than the apologetic, convincing someone of the validity of a theological position. Preaching has the ability through the music of language to transport you back into Bible times and enable you not only to see Moses at the burning bush but to be there yourself. To stand on holy ground yourself.

I remember one of the first sermons I heard by Gardner Taylor, called "Holy Ground." I got a sense for how a message is set up. How you don't show your hand too quickly. How you don't tell the story right away. In fact, Taylor does not actually mention the name Moses until about ten minutes into the sermon. In those days I had a phenomenal memory. Almost everything I heard I could remember, and so it was like programming a computer. It was a wonderful experience of capturing the beauty of language and the power of preaching.

C. D. Brooks also had a tremendous impact on my life. He was a very young preacher when I was first exposed to his preaching. I saw in him, and in Charles Bradford, very creative preaching. They made the Word of God come alive. Brooks would preach sermons like "The Age of Methuselah" and "The Virtue of Being Chicken," and you would have to ask, "What in the world is he going to talk about?" I just marveled at his creative ability.

Bradford had an amazing ability to tell a story. It was like sitting down and watching a movie. I learned the importance of dialogue in preaching. Not simply talking about what people say but letting them say it. These were my mentors—some formal, official mentors and some unofficial mentors. Leon Cox was my pastor for several years when I was in my teens, and he took a special interest in me. In fact, he took a number of us under his wing. He would invite us home and say, "What did you think about the appeal?" And then he would mention books to read. There was an intentionality to what he was doing. He was one of the smoothest preachers. He had a wonderful vocal instrument.

I remember a sermon he preached called "The Cup." His first passage was the one that described Joseph placing his cup in the sack of Benjamin. Then he moved over to the New Testament where Jesus said to James and John, "Can you drink of the cup?" So I learned how to use parallel and related passages in the construction of sermons and be more creative in my homiletical structures.

Calvin Rock, an outstanding preacher, also mentored me. He invited anyone who was interested in becoming a preacher to spend time with him during a week of prayer at Pine Forge Academy. He talked with us about preaching and poured out his heart.

So, long before I ever read a homiletics book or was exposed to preaching literature, I was being programmed.

When I finally started reading the literature, it awakened in me what was already there, half asleep in my own consciousness. Intuitively I had picked up on these things, caught these things, and so I found myself validating the literature or disagreeing with it based on what I had seen work in the crucible of human experience.

DM: What a blessing! And what a challenge to us as preachers to have a part in mentoring the next generation of preachers! In your own comments about preaching, you have spoken about "preaching out of the overflow." What are some of the ways you have of being filled up so you can preach out of the overflow?

BB: I get through the entire Bible three or four times a year. The way I do this is I listen to Scriptures. I have a 45-minute to one-hour commute to get to the Capitol. That gives me an opportunity to listen to CDs of the Scriptures. Right now I'm listening to the New International Version. You can listen to the Bible in 70 hours—the complete Bible! When I'm commuting, or when I'm flying on an airplane, I always have the Word in my CD player. I keep a pad of paper on my passenger seat, and although I'm not listening to find sermons, sermons find me! Fifty lifetimes would not be enough to preach out of that amazing reservoir of Scripture.

I get enough sermon material for five to six sermons a week easily. So I am constantly being fed from the Word. It's an amazing experience. It's something I look forward to. I can't wait to get in the car because I'm going to listen to the Word! You receive so much wonderful material when you expose yourself to the Word. Then, when you get up to preach, you are literally preaching out of the overflow.

DM: I've noticed you quote Scripture from memory when you're preaching. What process do you follow for hiding God's Word in your heart?

BB: I was blessed by being exposed to the Word when I was young. We were poor. We didn't have a TV, so we were in the Word, and we were in the church. My mother gave me my allowance based on learning my memory verses! So from five or six years old, my siblings and I memorized Scripture. I just love the Word. I listen, and I remember. Occasionally, there will be a passage of Scripture of such beauty that I write it down a couple of times, and then I can remember it. But in general, I just love to listen to the Word.

DM: What is the place of prayer in your preparation and delivery of sermons?

BB: I cannot preach without praying. I cannot study without praying. I cannot live without praying. I had a dramatic experience with the Lord 15 or 16 years ago, which took my spiritual life to another level. It took me to the place where I began to be aware of the constant presence of God. So I talk to Him! He is my Companion. He is there. And He talks to me.

That experience had a transforming impact on my personal life and on my preaching. When I get up in the morning, before my feet touch the floor, I swing out of bed on my knees. From that moment on, there are not many seconds of the day that I am not aware of the blessed presence of my Companion.

That's what prayer is all about. First Thessalonians 5:17 says, "Pray without ceasing." Each morning when I open the United States Senate with prayer, I am praying while I am praying. And when I am preaching, I am praying while I am preaching. While I'm going along, I'm receiving instructions, I'm receiving guidance, I'm practicing the presence of God. That's what prayer is to me. Prayer is not just something you do. It's something that permeates who you are.

DM: You mentioned that you pray while you are preaching. How does the Holy Spirit instruct you and guide you while you are preaching?

BB: I want to be in serious contact with God before I stand up to preach. I describe that as the "pray yourself hot" portion of sermon preparation. You can study yourself full and think yourself clear, but then you need to pray yourself hot! Without the Spirit of God, you are not going to be able to accomplish anything. Ask the Holy Spirit to go before you, to make this message live.

Enter the pulpit prepared to be used in whatever way the Spirit of God desires to use you. You should be so connected and so focused that when you step into the pulpit, you are ready for delivery! It is critically important that a preacher not try to use the Holy Spirit. We need to trust the Spirit of God to have His way, and to realize that the Spirit manifests Himself in different ways. But while the Spirit blows where He wants to, we have to learn how to set the sail. It's important to learn how to ride the wind.

Some preachers waste an awful lot of energy trying to be the wind instead of learning to sense what the Spirit is doing in a worship setting and cooperating with the Spirit. The preacher is simply a flute through which the Spirit of God is passing to make His music and touch the lives of His people.

DM: That's a beautiful concept! To what extent should preachers be transparent about their own spiritual journey, including their struggles and challenges?

BB: I would encourage judicious self-disclosure. It can be very therapeutic to share how God has enabled you to meet a specific struggle or challenge. One of my favorite Bible passages is in 2 Corinthians 1 where Paul says, "Blessed be the God and Father of our Lord Jesus Christ, the Father of mercies and God of all comfort, who comforts us in all our tribulation, that we may be able to comfort those who are in any trouble, with the comfort with which we ourselves are comforted by God" (2 Cor. 1:3, 4).

I hear in that passage that there is an appropriate place for judicious self-disclosure. I think the preacher has to be very careful in the use of personal illustrations. I don't like personal illustrations in which I'm the hero. But I find self-deprecating illustrations are very helpful. I talk sometimes about the struggle I had with profanity, growing up in the inner city. I picked up that habit. I wrestled with it. When I share about that struggle, people see that the minister is a human being, and they hear that the grace of Christ can liberate us from the chains that shackle us. That kind of revelation, the kind that brings glory to Jesus Christ and what He is able to do—that is the kind of personal illustration I would encourage preachers to use.

I would discourage preachers, particularly those who have had a prodigal-son pigpen experience, from making a career talking about what happened in the far country.

DM: What encouragement would you give to preachers who are feeling spiritually depleted?

BB: I would encourage preachers to expose themselves to the Word of God in as many creative ways as possible. It's that Word that ultimately brings us out of the fog. We do not live by bread alone but by every word that proceeds from the mouth of God. It was a word from the Lord that straightened up Moses time and time again. It was a word from the Lord that got Elijah back on track when he was suicidal. It's the Word that clears up the misconceptions—it's the manna. For me, the sweeping view of Scripture that you get from listening to the Bible multiple times per year is a tonic like nothing else I know. That will bring a harvest.

Second, I would encourage preachers to expose themselves to the fellowship of other ministers. There are some wonderful ministerial conferences that take place around the world every year. Going to a conference designed to build us up can be a wonderful tonic.

And third, if you don't already have a friend to whom you are accountable, preferably another minister, with whom you can be transparent, someone who can pray with you and for you, I would recommend that you find one. The Bible says that one will chase 1,000. Two will chase 10,000. There is a synergy and an energy in that kind of relationship that will help you in those plateau experiences, those arid wilderness experiences that we inevitably go through.

DM: What counsel would you leave with preachers who long to experience a deeply spiritual ministry so they can preach out of the overflow?

BB: I used to be frustrated with great preachers when I would ask them what made them so strong. It seemed to me they didn't take my question seriously. They talked about the importance of taking time with the Word of God, and that seemed so pedestrian to me, so boring. But the longer I live, the more I realize they were telling me the truth. We need to put the time in, exposing ourselves to the Word of God. Sermons are born there. But more than that, as we take time with the Word of God, we are born anew on a daily basis.

~

CHAPTER 4 — REFLECTION/DISCUSSION QUESTIONS

1. Take some time to reflect on your own spiritual journey. Who were the significant spiritual mentors in your life?

2. In order to preach out of the overflow, you need to be spiritually filled on a daily basis. What are some of the ways that you open your life to be filled by God?

3. What changes will you make in your life as a result of reading this chapter?

Notes:
1. "Preaching out of the Overflow." An interview with Barry Black, *Ministry* March 2004. Reprinted by permission.

FIVE
PRAYER-SATURATED PREACHING

Alvin VanderGriend is a leader in the Christian prayer movement and has written several books on prayer, including Love to Pray: A 40 Day Devotional for Deepening Your Prayer Life[1] and The Joy of Prayer: A 40-Day Devotional to Invigorate Your Prayer Life.[2] He is cofounder, along with Henry Blackaby, of the Denominational Prayer Leaders Network and a member of the National Prayer Committee in the United States.

DEREK MORRIS (DM): When did you first realize the importance of prayer?[3]

ALVIN VANDERGRIEND (AV): I was taught to pray from childhood. My parents encouraged me to pray when I got up in the morning and when I went to bed at night. They led us in prayer before and after each meal. I am deeply grateful for what I learned about prayer through my Christian upbringing. Some important foundations were laid.

But there was a lot about prayer I didn't know. I didn't know that prayer was all about relationship, a love relationship with God. I didn't know I had to ask for spiritual blessings in order to receive them. I didn't know what a difference intercession could make.

When I was ten years old, sitting in the balcony of our church, I was convicted that if I ever became a preacher, I would emphasize prayer. Several years later, when a senior in high school, I entered a speech contest for our church's youth convention and decided to speak about prayer. During my ministry, I was deeply moved by reading *Power Through Prayer* by E. M. Bounds. He emphasized that "in every truly successful ministry prayer is an evident and controlling force."[4]

DM: I have also appreciated *Power Through Prayer* by E. M. Bounds. Some have called that the greatest book on prayer ever written. Unfortunately, in my training, there was little or no training in regards to prayer or prayer ministries. Few understood about prayer-saturated lives, prayer-saturated preaching, and prayer-saturated churches. A lot of dangerous assumptions were made. Perhaps that is why Bounds, even in his day, asserted that "a school to teach preachers how to pray, as God counts praying, would be more beneficial to true piety, true worship, and true preaching than all theological schools."[5]

AV: I believe our seminaries should not assume that pastors in training understand prayer or that they are devoted to prayer. We need to lay a proper foundation for prayer-saturated ministry by teaching the Scriptures. I was amazed to discover that the Bible is over ten percent prayer. We need to recognize the place of prayer in the Scriptures and in the lives of the great heroes of faith. All the great heroes of faith were also heroes of prayer.

It's important to realize prayer doesn't start with us. Prayer starts with God. God is the Initiator. He moves us to pray. He gives us prayer ideas. He holds out the promises that we claim in prayer. God is at work in all our praying.

DM: You have noted in your writings on prayer that the early Christians, preachers in particular, were devoted to prayer.

AV: Prayer was a priority in the early Christian church. The prayers at their prayer meetings were not short, shallow, bless-me kind of prayers. They were truly devoted to prayer. Their leaders were devoted to prayer. The word devoted literally means "to occupy oneself diligently with something" or "to persist in." We read in Acts 6:4 that the apostles gave up other duties in order to devote themselves to prayer and the ministry of the Word. When I first read that passage, I asked myself this question: Where did the apostles learn to devote themselves to prayer and the ministry of the Word? The answer is obvious: they had been with Jesus.

They learned it from what they saw. They learned it from what they heard. Jesus spent entire nights in prayer. He bathed the key moments of His life in prayer. His words, His miracles, His power all came through prayer. The first Christians simply continued with what they saw in Jesus' life and heard from His lips. I'm convinced the amazing growth that took place in the early Christian church happened because of prayer-saturated lives and prayer-saturated preaching.

Bounds was right when he observed that "God's true preachers have been distinguished by one great feature: ...prayer.... God to them was the center of attraction, and prayer was the path that led to God."[6]

DM: What have you learned about the importance of prayer specifically as it relates to the preparation and delivery of powerful biblical sermons?

AV: The most important preparation is the preparation of the preacher. That has to happen in relationship with God, and prayer is an important part of that love relationship. By prayer, we invite the Holy Spirit to touch our hearts and lives, to impress us with the truths of a passage. The sermon needs to be born of prayer and bathed in prayer. The Holy Spirit knows the needs of my listeners, and He will reveal to me the things they need to hear. Then when we deliver the sermon, the Holy Spirit comes in response to our prayerful invitation and anoints us with power and freedom.

Bounds puts it this way, "Prayer, in the preacher's life, in the preacher's study, in the preacher's pulpit, must be a conspicuous and an all-impregnating force and an all coloring ingredient."[7] He continues, "The text, the sermon, should be the result of prayer. The study should be bathed in prayer, all its duties impregnated with prayer, its whole spirit the spirit of prayer."[8]

DM: That is powerful! Now tell us about the listeners. What is the role of the congregation in prayer-saturated preaching?

AV: Once I realized the importance of prayer for the preparation and delivery of powerful biblical sermons, I encouraged my listeners to pray for me. I agree with Bounds that "it is an absolute necessity that the preacher be prayed for."[9] I came across a quote by Frank Laubach in his book, *Prayer: The Mightiest Force in the*

World, that deeply moved me. This is what he said: "In nearly all congregations where we plead for every listener to pray hard we feel a strange, strong, delightful response from all parts of the room. Always, when congregations pray with great earnestness and unanimity, we feel lifted almost as though an invisible arm held us up; our hearts burn, tears lie close, and ideas come fresh and far better than any written address. Commonplace truth becomes incandescent, and burns like liquid metal. A congregation is three-fourths of a sermon!"[10]

Laubach continues, "Pastors around the world in ever increasing numbers are testifying that their preaching has been transformed by asking people to lean forward and pray."[11] That quotation just gripped me and confirmed my own experience that a prayer-saturated congregation makes a significant difference when I preach. When people in a congregation pray, something also happens for them! Their own hearts are brought under the authority of the Word. They are transformed from sit-and-soak listeners into giving and reproducing Christians. Their praying helps in that transformation. Prayer-saturated listeners are also impacting the people around them. A lot of good things happen when people devote themselves to prayer during the preaching of the sermon.

DM: So a preacher who is committed to prayer-saturated preaching would want to educate the congregation about the importance of prayer?

AV: Very much so! There is a church in Chino, California, that gives about twenty people who attend the worship service a "pray through" card. This card invites them to be designated prayers throughout the worship service. That's one way we can train members. We would like every listener to be devoted to prayer, but by selecting a certain number of designated prayers each week, we can educate our congregation about the importance of saturating the service with prayer.

DM: As you look back over your ministry, both as a local pastor and as a prayer leader, what is it that confirms for you the importance of prayer?

AV: There was a time in my ministry when I was functioning alone. The Holy Spirit led me to four other men; we covenanted to meet together for one to two hours every week to pray for each other. As we prayed for each other, I experienced a huge lift in my whole ministry, including my preaching.

Once I became a denominational prayer leader, I visited churches that were strong in prayer. After I visited about six of these churches, it dawned on me that every church that was strong in prayer was essentially healthy—impacting its community and growing through evangelism. One pastor gave this testimony: "When we work, we work; when we pray, God works!"

I have also seen prayer impact whole communities. When I was serving as a pastor in Chicago, we prayed fervently that God would show us a way to impact our community. I can still remember the prayer team kneeling in a circle in the living room of one of our members. They prayed passionately for about half the meeting time and the other half our time was spent discussing ways to impact the community for Christ. Out of that effort came a ministry to children called Story Hour that brought eighty-five neighborhood children to our church building each week. Then we offered Bible study opportunities to mothers who brought their children. Those mothers brought other mothers, which led to an evangelistic Bible study ministry that resulted in many people coming to Christ. That Bible study ministry has now become an interdenominational ministry. All of that community impact flowed out of prayer.

DM: Tell me about your efforts to encourage other pastors to devote themselves to prayer.

AV: We put together a prayer leadership team. The first meeting we prayed for a couple hours—and then we worked. The second meeting we prayed for a whole morning—and then we worked. The third meeting we prayed the whole day and then worked the second day. Out of that prayer leadership team came *The Praying Church Sourcebook*.[12] It was one of the first sourcebooks on prayer. It included twenty-seven different strategies that churches were using to grow and strengthen prayer in their churches, along with many stories and illustrations.

DM: That sourcebook is an amazing resource. I appreciate the practical suggestions, such as houses of prayer and the pastors' prayer team. What are some other ways that you have encouraged pastors and their congregations to devote themselves to prayer?

AV: We developed Lighthouses of Prayer, little groups of Christians praying in their homes and their churches. They focused on praying for hurting and unsaved people they knew in their workplaces and in their neighborhoods. As a result, the Lighthouse Movement developed, teaching thousands of people to pray particularly for the unsaved. We are continuing that emphasis in our 40 Days of Prayer initiative, which helps a whole church get lifted in its prayer life through prayer-saturated preaching, small groups, and prayer events.

DM: I understand you were also involved in the formation of the Denominational Prayer Leaders Network.

AV: That started back in 1989 with about fifteen denominational prayer leaders. At one point, we tabulated the number of local churches that were served by the leaders who were present and discovered, to our amazement, we represented about one hundred forty thousand churches! This group has met at least annually to pray together, encourage each other, and share resources and strategies. We find each time we gather together we are strengthened in our efforts as denominational prayer leaders as we try to help our congregations grow stronger in prayer and be Houses of Prayer.

DM: Can we expect a revival of prayer in the days ahead?

AV: Peter Wagner once said that the prayer movement was out of control. By that, he meant the prayer movement is out of our control and under the control of the Holy Spirit. There have been a lot of roadblocks, a lot of resistance, but there is still a growing interest in prayer. I believe prayer is the key to a revival of the church and the church's ministry and mission.

DM: What appeal would you make to each reader?

AV: We have to begin with ourselves. Ask the Holy Spirit to give you a holy discontent with the status quo, with maintenance-oriented Christianity. Ask for a spiritual hunger that you might long for the presence of God, the breaking in of God. We must be poor in spirit, beggars before the Lord. If we start there, the Lord is eager to answer that prayer. Beyond that, we have to become part of a praying community. Vital, powerful praying happens in a context with other believers. Jesus, in Matthew 18, encouraged corporate prayer and gave some promises in that regard. In the book of Acts, there are at least thirty-three references to prayer, twenty-six of which are references to corporate prayer. God's Word pictures a church devoted to prayer, persisting in prayer, and occupied diligently with prayer. That is what Jesus taught. That is what the New Testament church modeled. That is what God still expects today.

~

CHAPTER 5 — REFLECTION/DISCUSSION QUESTIONS

1. Who has been a model for you of a prayer-saturated life?

2. How can prayer become a more important part of your sermon preparation and delivery?

3. How can you help your listeners realize the importance of prayer as part of their personal and corporate worship experience?

Notes:

1. Alvin VanderGriend, *Love to Pray: A 40 Day Devotional for Deepening Your Prayer Life* (Terre Haute, IN: Prayershop Prayershop Publishing, 2007).

2. Alvin VanderGriend, *The Joy of Prayer: A 40-day Devotional to Invigorate Your Prayer Life* (Terre Haute, IN: Prayershop Prayershop Publishing, 2007).

3. "Prayer-Saturated Preaching." An interview with Alvin VanderGriend, *Ministry* July 2009. Reprinted by permission.

4. E. M. Bounds, *Power Through Prayer* (Grand Rapids, MI: Baker Book House, 1972), 38.

5. Ibid., 25.

6. Ibid., 41.

7. Ibid., 32.

8. Ibid., 40, 41.

9. Ibid., 109.

10. Frank C. Laubach, *Prayer: The Mightiest Force in the World* (New York, NY: Fleming H. Revell, 1946), 33, 34.

11. Ibid., 34.

12. Alvin VanderGriend and Edith Bajema, *The Praying Church Sourcebook* (Grand Rapids, MI: Church Development Resources, 1990).

SIX
THE WITNESS OF PREACHING

Thomas G. Long is a distinguished teacher and author in the field of preaching. He taught for many years at Princeton Theological Seminary before assuming his present position as the Bandy Professor of Preaching at Candler School of Theology. He has written and edited numerous books on preaching, including The Witness of Preaching, Preaching and the Literary Forms of the Bible, and The Senses of Preaching. Dr. Long has been recognized as one of the twelve "most effective preachers in the English-speaking world."

DEREK MORRIS (DM): In your many years of teaching and writing, you have made a compelling case for viewing the Christian preacher as a witness.[1] I wonder if we could begin by exploring that idea.[2]

THOMAS LONG (TL): Well, I'm attracted to that image for many reasons, not the least of which is that it's a New Testament image. As such, it has a double meaning: as witness and as martyr. It shows that the stakes are high for preaching the gospel, and the risk is great. Anytime we think it's safe to preach the gospel, we either misunderstand the gospel or we misunderstand the culture, because it's never safe to preach the gospel. There are always costs involved, and the martyr image makes that clear.

DM: How does this image of the Christian preacher as a witness affect our understanding of the preacher?

TL: First of all, it makes it clear the preacher does not stand there with something he or she has generated out of his or her own mind or competence. One's witness is always dependent upon something else. One bears witness about something or to something. Second, this image of a witness makes it clear that what is at stake is truth. Witness is a legal term. The person who has seen and experienced something the public needs to know for the sake of the truth is put on the stand, sworn in, and commissioned to do one thing: to tell the truth, the whole truth, and nothing but the truth, so help them God. And there is a great penalty for bearing false witness because we, the public, need to know the truth. The culture needs to know the truth about God and humanity, and the witness is telling that truth, the whole truth, and nothing but the truth.

DM: That sounds like a solemn responsibility, not one to be taken lightly. How should this call to be a witness affect the preacher?

TL: It should remind the preacher not to fudge the testimony, not to try to make it more palatable, more attractive, more acceptable. Sometimes the truth is hard to hear, but our commission is to tell the truth. It also helps us understand this very thorny issue of character, the moral character of the preacher. Sometimes you'll read in homiletical textbooks that the preacher must be of an exemplary moral character. People don't believe the message unless the preacher is one, two, or ten notches above the ordinary hearer. Other times, you read the ethical life of the preacher has no consequence whatsoever. The witness image balances those nicely in that, yes, the preacher must be a morally trustworthy person to the extent that the witness is willing to tell the truth. The totality of the moral life is important, but here it is not the essential issue. The central issue instead is the willingness of the witness, in this one place, not to hedge, not to fudge, to tell the truth about what has been seen and experienced. So those are some of the things that helped me reach out to this witness image as a provocative image for preaching.

DM: You emphasize, in your book *The Witness of Preaching,* that "the witness image carries with it guidance about the rhetorical form of preaching,"[3] and that "the shape of the witness's sermon should fit the character of the testimony."[4] How does the content of the testimony affect the form of the sermon?

TL: The problem in homiletics is that our field has a tendency to latch onto a particular form as the solution to our communication problems. So whether it's the three-point form, the narrative form, or the inductive form, you'll find people saying whatever we used to do is passé, what we now need to do is this or that. The witness image rejects a single form as the solution to a communication problem and recognizes that multiple rhetorical forms are available.

You don't, however, just pick them arbitrarily. You pick the one fitting for the kind of testimony you're giving. Sometimes the prosecuting attorney or the interrogating attorney will say to a witness, "Would you tell your story?" Well, that calls for a narrative form. The witness narrates the experience that embodies the testimony. Other times the prosecutor will want to know about particular facts. "What happened here? Was it day or night? Was the car blue or green?" So the communication of specific concrete factual information becomes the chosen rhetorical form. If you look at courtroom testimony, it takes hundreds of different styles, each one fitted to the information being communicated.

DM: You suggest that "the witness is not a neutral observer."[5] Is the witness permitted to share his or her own experience with the truth as part of the testimony?

TL: Your question is an apt one, and there is a tightrope to walk here. The court is not interested in the interior experiences and feelings of any witness. There is something the witness has seen and experienced and is telling about. So the truth we're after is outside of the witness. But in the case of the gospel truth, this is momentous and urgent truth. It's something like a witness in a court room who has seen a multi-car collision on the highway. He or she is bearing testimony to something that happened on the interstate that day. The fact that the accident was actually seen by them means they are now personally involved in it. There is no way for a true witness to be detached from what they've seen and experienced. This is encapsulated in Peter and John's passionate reaction to the order to stop preaching, that is, bearing witness in Jesus' name: "'We cannot help speaking about what we have seen and heard'" (Acts 4:20, NIV). So when we are bearing testimony, bearing witness to the gospel, we're always revealing our own involvement in the truth we are proclaiming.

Does that mean preachers can only preach things they have totally experienced?

The answer is no. The best image I know to illustrate that comes from an old Joseph Sittler sermon called, "The View from Mount Nebo," in which he develops the image of Moses on Mt. Nebo looking over into the Promised Land.[6] He can see it, but he will not experience it and there are many things in the gospel the witness can see but has not, in his or her own personal Christian maturity, fully experienced.

DM: You suggest that the witness of preaching must be viewed as part of "a great and cosmic trial." Does the witness of preaching have cosmic implications?

TL: Yes! Most Christian witness takes place in the context of corporate worship, and corporate worship is never understood theologically as just a little tiny congregation gathered for worship. We're gathered in the great company of saints at the Lord's great banquet table. Richard Fenn, who teaches at Princeton, has made the case—and I think it's a compelling one—that the structure of worship in most Christian communities is a kind of mock trial in which the charges are brought against God's people.[7] Then testimony is brought in, and the great acquittal, the announcement that in Jesus Christ there is no condemnation. That's good news! It's *the* Good News!

DM: What are the greatest challenges facing a preacher as a witness in the twenty-first century?

TL: Let me point to a couple: one in culture and one inside the church. Out in the culture, we have to negotiate a hearing everywhere we go. *The New York Times* is not going to print summaries of the sermons of the great New York preachers as they did a century ago. The culture is not interested in what preachers have to say. Therefore, in ways that are reconciling and peacemaking on the one hand, while they are disruptive and prophetic on the other, the preacher has to get out there in the public square and negotiate a hearing for the gospel. That's a terrific challenge.

Inside the church, I have been concerned at the loss of theological and biblical knowledge on the part of the average lay person. Preaching is an active ministry by the preacher, but theologically it is an act of the whole church. Therefore, preaching is not simply a person who knows something standing in front of people who don't know something and spilling out information. When we preach the gospel, we preach it to people who have heard the gospel, and it confirms what they have heard and stretches them to a new place, and back and forth it goes. One of the challenges for the preacher in the twenty-first century is to rebuild and refresh the memory of the church. Preachers need to give congregations their Bibles back, to rebuild their theological vocabulary, one brick, one word, one concept, one text at a time. And when seekers come in the door of the church, we should not suspend our vocabulary, our language, our lore, our stories, our gospel. We should teach it.

DM: What closing word of counsel would you give to a preacher who desires to be a faithful witness?

TL: The most important moment in the sermon creation process is what the old rhetoricians called the moment of invention, what the biblical hermeneuticians called the moment of interpretation, and what a homiletician might call the moment of encounter with the text. When a preacher will reserve the time and energy to dwell long enough, and energetically enough, on the text, so he or she arrives at that place where the text speaks, then the preacher has something to say. All the rest of the process is important, but not nearly as important as that. If there is not that moment, then all the wonderful illustrations, terrific structures, and charismatic personality in the world will not make this an authentic event. Responding to that, I'm really talking about a moment of hearing the voice of God in the text. Then you stand in the pulpit and say, "I just have to tell you what I have seen and heard."

~

CHAPTER 6 — REFLECTION/DISCUSSION QUESTIONS

1. What thoughts and emotions do you experience when you think of yourself as a witness in a "great and cosmic trial"?

2. Reflect for a moment on your own preaching ministry. How credible is your testimony as a witness for Jesus Christ?

3. How can preachers find the courage to tell the truth no matter what the cost?

Notes:

1. Thomas G. Long, *The Witness of Preaching* (Louisville, KY: Westminster/John Knox Press, 1989), 42-47.

2. "The Witness of Preaching." An interview with Thomas G. Long, *Ministry* July 2001. Reprinted by permission.

3. Thomas G. Long, *The Witness of Preaching* (Louisville, KY: Westminster/John Knox Press, 1989), 46.

4. Ibid.

5. Ibid.

6. Edmund A. Steimle, Morris J. Niedenthal, and Charles L. Rice, *Preaching the Story* (Philadelphia, PA: Fortress Press, 1980), 43-51.

7. Richard K. Fenn, *Liturgies and Trials* (New York: Pilgrim Press, 1982), 27; quoted in Thomas G. Long, *The Witness of Preaching*, 47.

SEVEN

PREACHING WITH PROPHETIC PASSION

Gardner C. Taylor is pastor emeritus of Concord Baptist Church of Christ, Brooklyn, New York. He has been recognized as one of the top twelve "most effective preachers in the English-speaking world."

DEREK MORRIS (DM): Dr. Taylor, in your Lyman Beecher lectures, you emphasize that "the preacher ought not dare to utter the things of Christ too hesitantly or casually or tentatively."[1] Why is it so important to preach with an earnest, honest passion?[2]

GARDNER C. TAYLOR (GT): I believe there are enough doubts in the congregation, and preachers have their own. We ought to hesitate to compound people's uncertainty. We are called to preach faith, not doubts.

DM: In your lecture on "Preaching the Whole Counsel of God," you assert that "if the watchman cannot see, or lacks clear vision, then the responsibility to preach should not be accepted."[3] Those are strong words. Are you saying if you can't preach with passion, you shouldn't preach at all?

GT: Yes! If we do not have insight into the human situation, with the healing of the gospel playing upon that situation, then we have no business preaching. Clear vision is crucial to the proclamation of the gospel.

DM: Some people would say it's rather audacious for us to preach with a prophetic passion, to call individuals, communities, or even nations to repentance, when we're just as sinful and faulty as the people we're addressing. How would you respond?

GT: Not only just as sinful; sometimes more so! I have been shamed times without number by the faith of people in my congregation, particularly in sickness, who seem to have a radiance, a confidence, and a certitude I wasn't sure I could have in that setting.

DM: So how should preachers deal with their uncertainties?

GT: I think we ought to be apologetic about those things of which we are uncertain. We ought to confess our own humanity and our own inability to believe complete-ly. I think preachers are overly presumptuous when they claim to be certain about everything. I remember going to a dear friend's home, a minister whose wife had just died. A young preacher came in loosely spouting assurances when hesitancy would have been better—maybe even silence. But to come in presumptuously talking with utter assurance when someone is passing through very deep waters is, I think, an insult.

DM: I hear you saying that while we may preach with prophetic boldness, we need to recognize we don't have all the answers. We must maintain a spirit of humility. In fact, you suggest that "touching and redeeming proclamation" cannot be uttered without a spirit of humility.[4]

GT: We all have much to be humble about. Looking at ourselves, at our own doubts, fears, our uncertainties, will give us a certain humility. When preaching the gospel, there is a temptation to pride. Of course, a family will help you greatly to keep some humility. When my daughter was younger, we took her to England and Scotland. One day I was scheduled to preach in Peterborough in the morning. My daughter wanted to play that afternoon. But I said to her, "Oh Martha, I don't feel like playing." She responded, "You don't ever want to play anymore." I felt accused and said, "Oh no, it isn't that. I have to preach in the morning." "And I have to listen to it!" she replied.

DM: That can keep you humble!

GT: Oh yes! I must say another thing. When one sees the magnitude of the gospel and recognizes how partial and fragmentary our proclamation of the gospel is, that in itself should induce humility.

DM: One of the steps you mentioned as part of sermon preparation, which seems to demand a spirit of humility, is sitting silent before God. I can understand prayer and study in sermon preparation, but what does it mean to sit silent before God?

GT: I got that from reading Alexander McClaren, whose expository work I greatly admire. I think McClaren was the greatest expositor we've seen in the Christian community since the apostolic days. I really believe that. But he spoke of sitting silent before God. I conceive that to be not particularly reading, not formally praying, but opening ourselves to whatever God would say to us at the time. This is not easy, because the clamors around us are loud and the clamors within us are no less so.

DM: Another step in sermon preparation that seems very important to you, in addition to sitting silent before God, is the use of imagination. You mentioned you view your sermon more as a journey than a list of principles. How do you use your imagination as you think about conveying the Word of God in a passionate way?

GT: A preacher I know cautioned me that one ought not to just plunge into a text, but one ought to walk up and down the street on which a text lives, see what the neighbors are like, and what the sky is like. What is the atmosphere around the text? One needs to become, in a way of speaking, a part of what one is preaching. One of our great gifts is the gift of imagination; that we are able to place ourselves in situations by imagination. I think we have to do that. For instance, that night when Saul consulted the witch, what was the turmoil in this man's heart as he prepared for battle? We ought not to have too great a difficulty putting ourselves in that place.

DM: That somehow moves the sermon from being flat and colorless and makes it something more alive.

GT: And personal. Here again we are talking about passion. I think there is a certain manufactured passion that is cheap. True passion comes naturally when one enters into what is occurring, becomes a part of it. When you preach the parable of the prodigal son, think of leaving home. Think of how your parents must feel when you walk out on them. Being a parent, how do you feel? Being a child, walking out, how would you feel? Talk about that.

DM: These are practical insights. How do we go about finding mentors who can help us preach with prophetic passion?

GT: I strongly recommend *The Concise Encyclopedia of Preaching,* by William Willimon and Richard Lischer.[5] Next to what E. C. Dargan did in the early part of the twentieth century at Southern Baptist Seminary,[6] it is the best compendium of preaching through the ages that I have ever seen.

DM: It's worth reading?

GT: Yes, definitely! It not only has the needed biographical background information, but it has certain excerpts from sermons that the preacher did, along with brief treatises on the kind of theological setting the person worked in. It's a tremendous volume.

DM: It may help others catch the vision as they interact with the lives and sermons of great preachers.

GT: Indeed. Not to copy but to see how others went about it and to catch something of others' imaginativeness or approach to Scripture. I spent many hours reading the lives and sermons of great preachers. That helped me immeasurably.

DM: Let me turn to preaching with prophetic passion that which addresses not only individual needs but also the needs of the culture, the needs of a whole nation. What is the preacher's responsibility in confronting the maladies of the culture?

GT: The first thing one ought to do is not preach at people. I think one ought to be careful about censoring people and accusing people. This is a futile undertaking. It may also be a way of vindicating our own prejudices! We ought to recognize we are all sinners and come at preaching about social issues from the point of view of the gospel and not merely from our own limited viewpoint.

DM: So we look at the needs of the culture and we speak to them but not in a chastising or censorious way.

GT: Certainly not in a way of talking down, as if we sit in a lofty seat of judgment from which we lecture people.

DM: History records the stories of many great men and women of God who suffered because they were willing to preach with that kind of prophetic passion. What have you seen in your own experience?

GT: Dr. Martin Luther King, Jr., is an example of one who paid a high price for what he preached. And a high price is still to be paid, but we're not here to negotiate bargains out of life. We are here to be made into something God wants us to be. I don't think anybody with a healthy turn of mind courts criticism, trouble, persecution, personal rejection, or disaster. Sometimes we have to say as Luther said, "Here I stand. I can do no other."

DM: When you speak of a willingness to suffer, it reminds me of the words of Jesus in the Sermon on the Mount: "Blessed are you when people insult you, persecute you and falsely say all kinds of evil against you, because of me. Rejoice and be glad, because great is your reward in heaven, for in the same way they persecuted the prophets who were before you" (Matt. 5: 11-12, NIV).

GT: That aspect of the gospel we have neglected. The gospel and our preaching of it has been so affected by our surrounding culture and the standards of that culture—the popular standards of "success"—that we have often been unfaithful to our Lord.

DM: When we preach with a prophetic passion, we should be willing to suffer, but not go looking for trouble.

GT: We ought to be very reluctant to court suffering, but I don't think it ought to be the first consideration in our ministry. Our loyalty to Jesus Christ ought to be first. Let everything else come in behind that.

~

CHAPTER 7 — REFLECTION/DISCUSSION QUESTIONS

1. Think back over the preachers who have impacted your life and ministry. Which preachers have modeled for you what it means to preach with prophetic passion?

2. How do you respond to Taylor's comment that "if you can't preach with passion, you shouldn't preach at all"?

3. What is the difference between preaching with prophetic passion and exhibiting a critical and judgmental spirit in your preaching?

Notes:
1. "Preaching with Prophetic Passion." An interview with Gardner C. Taylor, *Ministry* September 1999. Reprinted by permission.
2. Gardner C. Taylor presented the 1975-1976 Lyman Beecher lectures at Yale. These lectures are published in *How Shall They Preach* (Elgin, IL: Progressive Baptist Publishing House, 1977). This book also contains a collection of Taylor's Lenten sermons.
3. Ibid., 79.
4. Ibid., 31.
5. William H. Willimon and Richard Lischer, eds. *The Concise Encyclopedia of Preaching* (Louisville, KY: John Knox/Westminster Press, 1995).
6. E. C. Dargan, *The Art of Preaching in the Light of Its History* (New York, NY: Doran, 1922).

EIGHT
BULLETS OR BUCKSHOT

Haddon W. Robinson is the Harold John Ockenga Distinguished Professor of Preaching at Gordon-Conwell Theological Seminary. He has earned an international reputation as an outstanding biblical preacher and teacher of homiletics. Robinson has authored numerous books and articles on preaching, including his best-selling text Biblical Preaching. He has been recognized as one of the top twelve "most effective preachers in the English-speaking world."

DEREK MORRIS (DM): In *Biblical Preaching,* you emphasize that "a sermon should be a bullet, not buckshot."[1] In other words, a sermon should present a single dominant idea rather than a collection of numerous unrelated ideas. In my preaching workshops, many pastors express the desire to understand the process of crafting a homiletical bullet. So perhaps we could explore that process together. Let's start with a working definition of biblical preaching.[2]

HADDON ROBINSON (HR): Biblical/expository preaching is the communication of a biblical concept, and that concept is derived from the historical, grammatical, literary study of a scriptural passage in its context. The Spirit of God takes that concept and makes it alive in the experience of the preacher, and through the preacher applies it to the people in the congregation. In other words, biblical preaching is the proclamation of a concept derived from Scripture.

DM: With that as a working definition, how does the preacher go about discovering the biblical concept in a passage?

HR: A preacher has to understand the Bible is a book of ideas. In order to discover the main idea of a passage, you need to ask two questions. "What is the writer talking about?" That's the *subject,* and it always answers a question—who, what, where, when, why, how. When you've answered that question and determined the subject of the passage, you ask, "What is the author saying about the subject?" That's the *complement.*

DM: So subject plus complement equals the biblical concept, the exegetical idea. Let's take Psalm 117 as an example and see how the process works: "Praise the Lord, all you nations; extol him, all you peoples. For great is his love toward us, and the faithfulness of the Lord endures forever. Praise the Lord" (verses 1, 2).[3] First, we ask what the psalmist is talking about. If one says the psalmist is talking about "praise," or about "the Lord," how would you respond?

HR: Yes, the psalmist is talking about praise, but the passage is not telling you everything about praise. It's not telling *where* or *when* you should praise the Lord. What it is talking about is *why* you should praise the Lord.

DM: So the subject would be: *why everyone should praise the Lord.*

HR: That's right. The psalmist says, "Praise the LORD, all you nations; extol him, all you peoples. For great is his love toward us, and the faithfulness of the LORD endures forever." The complement, therefore, is *because His love and faithfulness endure forever.*

DM: Discovering the exegetical idea in that short passage of Scripture is perhaps simple because we've basically restated the text. But it becomes a little more complicated when you move into a larger passage of Scripture. Let's consider Luke 15. That's a familiar preaching passage. I suppose a preacher would have to determine whether to look at all three parables as a trilogy or just focus on one. What would you say?

HR: Whether you preach the whole passage or not, is not your question when you first study. The first question is, "What is it that Luke is trying to get at?" The opening verses of the chapter give you the subject. "Now the tax collectors and 'sinners' were all gathering around to hear him. But the Pharisees and the teachers of the law muttered, 'This man welcomes sinners and eats with them'" (verses 1, 2). The subject of the passage is the complete answer to the question, "What is the author talking about?" That is, *How can Jesus welcome tax collectors and sinners?*

DM: The rest of the passage completes that idea?

HR: Yes, the rest of the passage would be the complement. Verse 3 says, "Then Jesus told them this parable." That's singular. He tells them three stories: one about a lost sheep, another about a lost coin, and one about two lost boys. One parable, but three stories. Each of those stories is getting at a similar truth: God loves people, God seeks for people, God is merciful to people. In the last part of the parable, we have the elder brother, the key to the story in a sense. There are two audiences being addressed: the publicans and sinners, and the Pharisees and teachers of the law. In the part that deals with the elder brother, Jesus is obviously speaking about the Pharisees and teachers of the law. The elder brother is as lost as the younger brother because you can be lost in a foreign country or you can be lost in the father's house if you're out of sympathy with the father's heart. You're as lost as the boy who's gone off and wasted a fortune. But in each case, it really isn't the story about the lost sheep, the lost silver, or the lost sons. The story is about the seeking shepherd, the seeking woman, and the seeking and waiting father. In each of these stories, God is concerned about lost people because He loves them, values them, pities them. So that would be the complement to the passage and the answer to the subject question: *Because God is concerned about lost people.*

DM: Let me summarize what you've said. The subject of the passage is *"How can Jesus welcome tax collectors and sinners?"* And the complement is *"because God is concerned about lost people."* So the exegetical idea of the passage would be a combination of subject + complement: *Jesus welcomes tax collectors and sinners because God is concerned about lost people.* Once we have discovered that biblical concept, a combination of the subject and complement, does that become the homiletical bullet?

HR: Sometimes, but often it has to be restated. Some ideas, when you state them, are as applicable to people today as they would have been 2,000 years ago.[4] Other ideas are directed at the people of the first century because the biblical writer was talking about people in that age. Then you have to work with the exegetical idea and ask, "What does this mean to people today? How would I state it in terms that would be meaningful to the folks sitting in the pews?" And that's where your homiletical idea, or bullet, comes in.

DM: Let's look at another example. In Colossians 4:1 we read, "Masters, provide your slaves with what is right and fair, because you know that you also have a Master in heaven." Now if we're working the process you just described, we might suggest the subject of the text is, *"Why masters should provide their slaves with what is right and fair,"* and the complement would be *"because they know that they also have a Master in heaven."* But I'm not going to be able to preach that as it stands to a 21st century congregation. I can't just stand up and say, "Masters treat your slaves fairly because you know that you also have a Master in heaven." In itself that's ir- relevant in a culture in which there are no slaves!

HR: Right, because the difference between the first century and the 21st century is that we're not dealing with masters and servants. You could say masters could be employers and slaves could be employees. That isn't quite bringing it into the 21st century, but what is there in this text that would apply to those who work with people under them, and what motivation do they have to be just, right, and fair with people? The answer is if you're an employer, it's important to remember that God is your Master and therefore you should treat your employees as God treats you. So you might say, *"You ought to deal with people around you, that work for you, in a way that is right, just, and fair, because you don't work for yourself. You work for the Boss in heaven and you have to serve Him."*

DM: So in crafting the homiletical idea, you are staying as close to the exegetical idea as you can, but still wanting to make it relevant. Let's look at another passage to illustrate the process of restating the exegetical idea as a contemporary homileti- cal idea. 1 Corinthians 8 is a well-known passage about meat offered to idols. How would the exegetical idea of this passage be relevant to people in the 21st century?

HR: This passage speaks to a problem some people still face, because they still have to deal with the issue of food offered to idols. But it's not an issue in many countries of the world. So at first glance it would seem the passage would not have anything to do with us today because we don't have to deal with food offered to idols.

DM: So, I suppose we have two options at this point: delete the passage from our preaching calendar and choose another; or work the process and ask, "What is the subject? What is the complement? What is the biblical concept here, and how can I state that exegetical idea in a contemporary way?" Let's take the second option and work the process. What do you see as the subject of this passage?

HR: Paul states the subject in his opening comment: "Now about food sacrificed to idols." Of course, he's not telling us everything about food sacrificed to idols. I think what he's telling us or the question he's answering is, "How do you deal with the problem of whether or not to eat food sacrificed to idols?" He is saying in the passage there are two ways of coming at this. One is by knowledge, and knowledge would say you could eat anything offered to an idol, because an idol is nothing. Secondly, he says love for those who are weaker brothers and sisters is an important consideration. So if I were going to put it into a subject and complement, the subject is *"How Christians should deal with food offered to idols,"* and the complement is *"with knowledge, limited by love."* I think that's what Paul is saying in 1 Corinthians 8.

DM: So the exegetical idea would be *"Christians should deal with food offered to idols with knowledge, limited by love."* But let's say we're going to share this sermon in a setting where meat offered to idols is not an issue. What might we do with that exegetical idea, which seems locked in the first century, as we craft it into a homiletical bullet that will make an impact in the 21st century?

HR: I have to work with the exegetical idea and ask, "What is Paul dealing with when he talks about meat offered to idols?" You have to understand what this meant to people in Corinth 2,000 years ago. It was a social problem. At the center of the town was the temple to the goddess Aphrodite. People who went to worship Aphrodite brought a sacrifice. A part of the sacrifice was put on the altar, another part was given to the priest as an honorarium, and another part was given back to the worshipers so they would have a splendid meal as a result of the worship. So the question being asked was, "Could Christians eat the meat that had been offered to an idol?" Sometimes that was the only meat available in town. Or if an unbeliever invited them over to a feast on the day of worship, could they go and eat the food given them? Would there be a social problem? There's also a psychological problem, because some Christians were tied into idolatry, and this was part of the worship of idols. Thus it also became a spiritual problem for some people to eat meat offered to an idol.

When Paul was dealing with this issue, he was dealing with the questionable. He was not dealing with adultery, stealing, coveting, or bearing false witness. There's no question about these issues. In this passage, Paul was dealing with an issue that upset people. Thus the matter had spiritual overtones, but it was not directly prohibited in the Scriptures. So, in crafting the homiletical idea, I would have to ask, "Where do my people come up against similar questionable issues that they have to wrestle with?"

For example, a businessman said to me, "I work at a business, and we have conventions. Is it all right for me as a Christian to go to a party where they have an open bar and serve alcohol?" I can't answer that question as such from Scripture. So I would say to him, on one level, "Yes, there is nothing wrong in going to that party." But if he says to me, "I've got a fellow rooming with me who's a new Christian and a recovering alcoholic, and this really bothers him. Now is it all right for me to go?" That's a whole different question, because now you brought in a new believer who could be affected by your going.

Paul tells us that first of all, you have to act according to knowledge. By knowledge he means having a doctrinal understanding of why you are or are not doing something. Most of the time, if you really understand the Scriptures, you have a great deal of freedom. But then Paul says freedom must be limited by love. Because, he says, if a weaker brother sees you, then even though you know you can do it, and you feel perfectly free to do it, you don't do it out of love and consideration for that brother.

DM: How do we shrink that fairly lengthy discussion into a single dominant thought, a concise memorable bullet?

HR: I would say, *"Whenever you deal with issues that are questionable, you need to be sure you're operating on the basis of biblical knowledge; but that knowledge has to be limited or conditioned by love."* That's probably what I would use in my sermon.

DM: When the congregation leaves at the end of the sermon, we know the listeners will not remember everything. But we're hoping at least they will remember the biblical concept, the single dominant thought. What are some ways we can drive home that homiletical idea?

HR: The homiletical idea should be clearly in my mind when I preach the sermon. I would try to state that idea as succinctly as possible, and I would probably repeat it eight or ten times in the sermon. When I come to the conclusion of the message, I want to leave them with that single focus. I want to conclude in such a way that people think about the homiletical idea.

DM: In a written document, you can use a colored marker to highlight a key idea. But colored markers don't work in oral presentations. What are some other ways to highlight that key idea besides making it as succinct as possible and repeating it?

HR: Well sometimes, I will actually flag it. I will say to people, "Now listen to the principle."

DM: You actually give your hearers an indication that this is the key issue.

HR: That's right. I could say, "Get hold of this, because this is the way you have to think if you're a Christian. Here's the principle." Then I would give it to them, and I would come back to it again, so they see the principle and how it works. If my congregation left and they said, "I wonder what in the world he was talking about this morning," I'd feel like I had failed. They may not remember the outline, but they ought to remember the bullet. What you're really doing is trying to discover great biblical truths and drive them home into peoples' lives.

~

CHAPTER 8 — REFLECTION/DISCUSSION QUESTIONS

1. Review the last sermon you preached or the last sermon you heard. Was the sermon a bullet or buckshot? State the main idea of the sermon in a single, memorable sentence. How can the preaching idea be improved?

2. Which preacher do you appreciate for his/her ability to craft a preaching idea in such a way that it sticks in the minds of the hearers?

3. What are some practical ways you can remind yourself of the importance of driving home a single dominant thought in each of your sermons?

Notes:

1. Haddon W. Robinson, *Biblical Preaching: The Development and Delivery of Expository Messages.* 2nd ed. (Grand Rapids, MI: Baker Academic, 2001), 35.

2. "Bullets or Buckshot?" An interview with Haddon Robinson, *Ministry* September 2000. Reprinted by permission.

3. All Scripture passages quoted in this chapter are from the New International Version.

4. Robinson notes that when the biblical concept found in the text is a universal principle, the wording of the homiletical idea may be identical to that of the exegetical idea. (Robinson, 104). For example, "pray without ceasing"—the exegetical idea of 1 Thessalonians 5:17—could also be used as a homiletical bullet. It is just as relevant to Christians in the 21st century as it was to the Thessalonian believers in the 1st century.

NINE
INDUCTIVE PREACHING

Fred B. Craddock (retired) was Professor of Preaching and New Testament at the Candler School of Theology. He has authored numerous books on preaching, including his best-selling text Preaching. *He has been recognized as one of the top twelve "most effective preachers in the English-speaking world."*

DEREK MORRIS (DM): In the past two decades, you have championed the cause of inductive biblical preaching.[1] What's behind such commitment?

FRED B. CRADDOCK (FC): The theological reasons have to do with the community and the Book, giving the listeners room to arrive at conclusions rather than concluding and then preaching on it. All Bible study that is good Bible study is inductive, so why not just do it that way in the pulpit? Some people don't like inductive methodology because it sounds like it doesn't have any authority to it. But it has more authority than deductive methodology. It's just that it is relocated between them and the Book.

DM: In your book, *As One Without Authority,* you suggest that if you do not allow your listeners to follow you in an inductive fashion, you have taken away their freedom to discover the truth.[2] What do you mean by that?

FC: It means you leave your listeners in that pitiful box of having only two alternatives of agreeing or disagreeing with you. It is all your work. It is all packaged and delivered. So you get to say, "I agree with you," or "I don't agree with you." But in inductive preaching, you unroll your idea in such a way that listeners have to work to get it themselves. I think it is a compliment to preaching when listeners don't quite know whether they thought it themselves or got it from something the preacher said!

DM: So it's not as though you have nothing to say. Rather, you are trying to invite the community to come with you to the Book.

FC: That's right! When I first started in the pulpit, I would give them my proposition at the beginning and then break it down into points. That was my sermon. Nobody asked me, "Where did you get that from?" I studied, I worked, but I started at the finish line. They were used to it so they didn't raise any questions. I was the one who raised the questions.

DM: It sounds like you came to the conclusion that you wanted to encourage the interaction to occur between your listeners and the Book. It was your desire to be a catalyst rather than a person who just stands up and explains or reports. Is there any danger with this inductive approach to biblical preaching?

FC: Some young preachers have taken the inductive method as an excuse for getting up and saying nothing, just being casual. I have been embarrassed by going to seminars where somebody gets up and says, "Since I read Craddock's book, I don't really prepare anything. I just kind-of toss out this and that." That gives me the shakes. I wanted to achieve just the opposite: careful Bible study.

DM: You have suggested the inductive process calls for incompleteness. How do you avoid frustrating or confusing your listeners? People want clarity and some definition, but you want to maintain a sense of anticipation. How do you determine your degree of incompleteness?

FC: That is a good question, and I cannot give an easy answer! I would say after preaching 8 out of 10 of my sermons, I go back and write notes to myself. "Went too far." "Didn't go far enough." If I am preaching to a group that is biblically alert and committed Christians, I can take them along an inductive path, and I will shortly find them ahead of me, sitting on the porch waiting! Other groups say, "Go ahead, please tell us what you are trying to say so we can go on to the cafeteria!" So your question is pastoral as well as theological and homiletical. You don't want to frustrate people; you don't want to ask ninety-nine questions and sit down. If you ask more than one question, you are asking too many. You may ask that one question several ways, some of them quite leading, but keep your focus. Don't let your listeners chase rabbits everywhere and then go home saying, "I don't know what in the world the preacher was talking about."

DM: It would seem that with inductive preaching, it is especially important to recognize the non-verbal cues of your listeners. Somehow you have to keep them right on the edge of discovery. How do you accomplish that?

FC: Yes, as you preach you are reading the listeners. You are sometimes pausing and being casual, what I call "stopping and sitting on a bench a minute." You can tell as you are speaking if you are making progress. Sometimes you jump in too deep. They can't swim. Then what are you going to do? Going back is just as dangerous as going forward. I usually carry a plan B!

DM: If a pastor is wanting to explore the inductive method, what suggestions would you offer?

FC: Most people who follow the inductive method are inductive up to a certain point. Then, near the end of the sermon, they start drawing some conclusions. It is something like an inductive opening and a deductive closing. If I were just starting, that is how I would start. In fact, I would make a practice of constructing my sermon to lead to that result.

DM: In other words, you would gently let your listeners know you will be expecting more active participation from them when they listen to the sermon. Is that it?

FC: Yes, that's right. It's expecting more of them, but you are not doing it all at once. They are learning to listen to you; you are learning to speak to them. When I started preaching inductively as the pastor of a church, people at the door would say, "Was that a sermon? That wasn't a sermon!" And I said, "Did you follow it?" "Well, some of it, but I didn't know what you were doing." So at a fellowship dinner, I told the people, "I expect more work out of you folks. Listening is hard work. I want you to draw some conclusions." We worked together, and we had a lot of fun. I made a lot of mistakes, but gradually they developed the ability to think about what I was saying, to think their own thoughts and remember things. I learned a great deal.

DM: I notice you have the ability to make your listeners laugh. You seem to establish rapport by looking at the humorous side of things.

FC: Laughter does that. It makes a community when everybody laughs together. It is liberating for both you and your listeners. Seriousness of purpose does not require heaviness of mind. You can be light on your feet and still be very serious about what you are doing. In my early days, I used to defeat myself with a counter-productive heaviness. If you don't give your listeners an opportunity to relax and chuckle, they will find an opportunity. But they will do it at the wrong time, when you are trying to be serious. In other words, if you don't let them up for air, they will come up for air at the wrong time!

DM: I hear you saying that when you preach inductively, it's good to plan resting points for your listeners. What other suggestions would you give to those who want to improve their preaching?

FC: I have learned if you say something really true and wise, it is layered. Even children will get your point, but on a different level than the parents. People will come back and say, "You know, I have been thinking about that." Life is layered, and I think truth is layered. When Jesus told the parables, I am sure some kids nudged each other, but they didn't really get it like some others did. So that is the way I think we should preach. And finally, don't try to pack too much into a sermon. If you put too much on the plate, they can't eat it all, and when they see they can't eat it all, they may quit eating altogether. Just say one thing; say it a lot of different ways. Weave it in and out of the text. One idea is enough.

~

CHAPTER 9 — REFLECTION/DISCUSSION QUESTIONS

1. If a preacher is following a purely inductive method, the preaching idea is never directly stated. Rather the listeners are encouraged to discover that main idea for themselves. Why is it still vitally important for the preacher to have a clear grasp of the simple, memorable idea of the sermon?

2. Under what conditions would inductive preaching be preferable to deductive methodology where the main idea of the sermon is clearly stated at the beginning of the sermon?

3. Narrative preaching is inductive. Why is narrative preaching so appealing to modern and post-modern listeners?

Notes:
1. "Inductive Preaching." An interview with Fred B. Craddock, *Ministry* July 1998. Reprinted by permission.
2. Fred B. Craddock, *As One Without Authority* (Nashville, TN: Abingdon, 1979), 62, 68.

TEN
PREACHING CHRISTIAN DOCTRINE

Marguerite Shuster is the Harold John Ockenga Professor of Preaching and Theology at Fuller Theological Seminary in Pasadena, California.

DEREK MORRIS (DM): Dr. Shuster, in both teaching and writing, you have become an advocate of preaching Christian doctrine.[1] Yet, in your essay entitled "Preaching the Trinity," you state: "I am well aware, then, that I am swimming against a powerful tide when I plead for a rebirth of doctrinal preaching."[2] Why is there such a resistance to preaching Christian doctrine?

MARGUERITE SHUSTER (MS): Many people are laboring under a rather stereotypical view of what doctrine is—that it is a matter of splitting hairs about material that is abstract, incomprehensible, and unconnected to daily life—and that you have to have several years of graduate education to know what the discussion is about. So as soon as people hear that you are pleading for the rebirth of doctrinal preaching, the responses range from anxiety, to terror, to flight!

DM: You share with your students that every preacher preaches some kind of doctrine, whether they do it well or not. So how do you define the kind of doctrinal preaching you are wanting to hear?

MS: Well, let me first reinforce the fact that most pastors do not avoid or neglect preaching doctrine because they have thought about it consciously. Every time we open our mouths, we express some kind of implicit understanding of what, let's say, our view is of human freedom over against divine sovereignty, or what the relationship of God's love is to God's wrath. Every time we say, "Trust Jesus," we're assuming there is something particular about Jesus. Otherwise, why not trust somebody else?

So everything we say relies in the end upon doctrine. My concern is that we not leave it all implicit, that we at least make our affirmations explicit. When I think of preaching Christian doctrine, I think of giving explicit attention to addressing the content and consequences of some aspect of Christian belief and its meaning from both an intellectual and practical point of view.

DM: Once preachers accept the challenge to preach Christian doctrine, you suggest one major challenge they will face is that "persons in the average congregation are stunningly ignorant of Christian fundamentals."[3] So how do you meet that challenge? You want to be faithful in preaching Christian doctrine, and yet you've got biblically illiterate people in your congregation.

MS: Yes, and to make it worse, we have enormously transient congregations. So it's very hard to build from week to week. If you had people you could count on being there over a period of time, you might actually be able to make some progress at the level of complexity. But that's not real life in most of our congregations.

I tell my students they need to start with a bite-size piece of doctrine that counts, and they will discover that people's taste for the material will grow. All preaching needs to be the kind of preaching that is sufficiently clear, so a person with minimal understanding—or even a child—gets something from the sermon. Those with greater comprehension will also find there are depths for them to plumb.

DM: So you've got to start with a bite-size piece, so even a person with little background can take that first step of understanding.

MS: Yes, in doctrinal preaching we need to make clear to people what we are talking about, whether we use technical vocabulary or not. We don't throw around high-flown words, we do deal with substance. In this way, people can grab hold and say, "Aha, so that's what this is all about!"

DM: Which raises another challenge. Besides the lack of biblical knowledge in our hearers, a lot of the vocabulary we preachers use when we speak on doctrinal issues is totally foreign to the hearer.

MS: As a matter of fact, doctrinal language is often also foreign to the preacher! For example, when you ask a person to preach a sermon on the atonement, that person first has to know what is involved in the word and in the concept of atonement. I don't think there is one preacher in twenty who can articulate that intelligently. That's one reason preachers are afraid to preach Christian doctrine.

DM: It sounds like you're asking for much more careful study in preparation for doctrinal preaching.

MS: I wish preachers valued the whole of their preparation more, including the whole of their seminary preparation in terms of their systematic theology and biblical studies. For me, all that should come together in the sermon. If pastors haven't been well grounded in the loci of systematic theology, they face tremendous hurdles. They can pick up a bit from dictionaries and so on, but it will feel superficial, and such pastors will feel as if they are skating on thin ice.

DM: What are some of the risks a preacher faces when preaching doctrine?

MS: One special temptation is that we want something we can nail down. We can put tremendous demands on preachers, and preachers can feel the pressure of those demands in such a way that they make everything too easy, too tidy.

There are, of course, some things about our faith that are, in some kind of fundamental way, simple. God does intend in Scripture to make Himself known. He is not playing hide and seek. We believe an honest reader without special education or special tools may receive what they need for salvation simply by reading God's Word. But that which is sufficient is in no way exhaustive. Mystery remains.

Many of God's ways remain hidden to us; and this fact is especially pressing for people when it comes to the problems of sin and evil. There is sin in their own lives with which they cannot deal effectively and finally. There is evil around them that involves not only the suffering of the innocent but also structural evil. Such things don't mesh easily with any kind of tidy and simple moralistic approach.

The other side is simply saying, "It's all a mystery," and throwing up one's hands; or else trying to play out every aspect of it in a way that becomes so complex that a person simply bogs down, leaving nothing that one can affirm, nothing upon which one can rely.

DM: Is it acceptable, then, to raise questions you don't have an answer for? You talk about the honest or thoughtful skeptic who might think it's a sign of failure to even ask a question. Could the preacher raise a question even if there isn't an easy answer for it?

MS: Absolutely. If preachers don't raise it, they are simply ignoring the fact that practically everybody in the congregation already has. That can make the people suppose the preacher lives in an entirely different world where this question has never occurred.

I will almost always raise difficulties in a sermon. I would hope there is something one can say beside the difficulties that helps to show a way forward, but that doesn't mean the difficulties are dissolved or cast aside. In fact, another danger is raising difficulties and then simply dismissing them as if they didn't matter. That's condescending, it's demeaning, it's undermining of a faithful person's integrity.

DM: Is there a difference between writing about Christian doctrine and preaching about it?

MS: Yes. For example, contrast Karl Barth's *Dogmatics* and his sermons. Even when Barth was preaching to a university crowd, as opposed to, say, when he was preaching to prisoners, the sermons have an emotive power, a basic simplicity, and a fundamental affirmation of Christian hope that can be taken in on a wide variety of levels—from the most primitive perception that there is help from someone named Jesus, to fairly sophisticated nuancing if one is familiar with the sweep of

Barth's theology. But the sermon itself doesn't sound anything like the *Dogmatics* even if one may find, as I do, that there is great devotional value in the *Dogmatics*.

DM: In your writings on preaching doctrine, you seem to differentiate between a thematic approach, where you try to cover everything the Bible says in 25 minutes, and the approach of taking a portion of Scripture and addressing the Christian doctrine upon which it sheds light. Can you unpack that for us?

MS: I came upon that approach when the late Paul Jewett was writing the first volume of his systematic theology and wanted to include doctrinal sermons.[4] He believed that there is something wrong with doctrine that can't be preached.

He asked me to take on the task of writing certain sermons that would in some way embody doctrinal themes. I found it to be doable, challenging, and exciting. If one tries to preach a sermon on "faith," one ends up saying almost nothing. C. S. Lewis once said, "Everything is a topic on which not much can be said."

If you're trying to cover too much, there really isn't any way of bringing it down to earth. But if you take a particular passage that might have to do with somebody's faith or somebody's doubt, you can explore that slice of it in a way that the hearer will say, "Ah, that's where I live my life."

For this to work well, the preacher needs to deal primarily with that piece, but she or he must also know where the piece fits. That's why I tell my students that, although I want them to base their sermon on the exegesis of the passage, I also want them to consult dogmatic works on the doctrine so the broader context that informs the way they shape the sermon will also be faithful to the whole.

DM: Is it appropriate, then, to draw on other passages of Scripture or should the preacher stay with one primary text?

MS: I do believe it's possible to use supporting texts in a responsible way. However, most of the time when I hear people do it, they get engaged in proof-texting. They don't take into account the actual context of the supporting pieces they're using. Or if they do, they start running off on rabbit tracks and preaching the other texts.

I would rather they be aware the other texts exist and that they not speak in a way that would embarrass them in the light of the other texts. Sometimes referring to other texts will simply be a way of the preacher raising in his or her own mind the kinds of questions and objections that an engaged group of hearers will have in their minds without necessarily running to a direct exploration of those passages.

DM: That's very practical counsel. Do you see the need for illustrative material in doctrinal preaching?

MS: It's absolutely critical. You don't have a sermon unless you have material that connects with both heart and head. Of course, the proportions may be different in different kinds of sermons. But any sermon that doesn't make a contemporary connection hasn't done most of what a sermon needs to accomplish.

Now, when I say "illustration," I don't necessarily mean an anecdote. There are lots of ways to provide the supporting material that will make plain the contemporary relevance of the piece. I'm not leaving out anecdotes. I just do not want to limit the ways in which we illustrate.

DM: How important is the task of writing a manuscript when preparing for doctrinal preaching?

MS: Karl Barth believed that writing out a manuscript was simply part of the discipline of preaching. You didn't necessarily bring it into the pulpit but it was part of the discipline. Many others, like Martin Marty, have said that at least for the first ten years of their ministry, they considered that writing out a manuscript was essential to the piece having coherence, integrity, and all those other things we want. But careful preparation does not necessarily dictate what one brings into the pulpit. Different preachers will make different choices in that regard.

DM: What are your recommendations regarding the specifics of sermon design when the pastor accepts the challenge of preaching doctrine?

MS: I counsel variety. If every time you preach a doctrinal sermon you've got three points and a poem or you pull out the overhead and put up something incomprehensible or hand out an outline for people to fill in, you send the signal that this is a head trip. So I counsel variety of form for all preachers.

I have three underlying rules for a sermon: it needs to be biblical, it needs to be interesting, and it needs to make sense. If it's not biblical, I don't think it's a sermon. If it's not interesting, I won't listen. And if it doesn't make sense, I can't follow it.

DM: How would you respond to the criticism that postmodern secular people just aren't interested in Christian doctrine?

MS: Well, first the preacher had better believe it's relevant. Then, the preacher needs to show in very concrete ways, how what we believe addresses, challenges, and subverts ordinary assumptions about human life; how it confronts us in our deepest distress as human beings; how it eases our darkest fears; how it adds new fears and concerns that maybe we hadn't known we ought to be anxious about.

Preaching may raise anxieties, of course, as well as alleviate them. Suppose we're saying that Jesus has something to offer. Why Jesus? You cannot answer that question without doctrine. So how do you express what you believe about Jesus in a way that does indeed connect with people's deepest needs?

Somebody who is threatened by drought may not be experiencing the same need as somebody who is worried about drive-by shootings. So the way you shape matters obviously depends on your context. But if we believe Jesus Christ is good news for all people, then it seems utterly incumbent upon us to find ways of talking about Him that are real for the real people we address.

~

CHAPTER 10 — REFLECTION/DISCUSSION QUESTIONS

1. What is the difference between doctrinal preaching as proposed by Marguerite Shuster and proof-text preaching?

2. How do you feel about raising difficult questions which are not easily answered?

3. What are some of the challenges you face when you preach Christian doctrine?

Notes:

1. "Preaching Christian Doctrine." An interview with Marguerite Shuster, *Ministry* January 2002. Reprinted by permission.

2. Marguerite Shuster. "Preaching the Trinity: A Preliminary Investigation," in *The Trinity: An Interdisciplinary Symposium on the Trinity.* Edited by Stephen T. Davis, Daniel Kendall, Gerald O'Collins. (Oxford, England: Oxford University Press, 1999), 372.

3. Ibid., 358.

4. Paul K. Jewett, *God, Creation, and Revelation: A Neo-Evangelical Theology: with sermons by Marguerite Shuster* (Grand Rapids, MI: William B. Eerdmans, 1991). See also Paul K. Jewett, *Who We Are: Oar Dignity As Human: A Neo-Evangelical Theology;* edited, completed, and with sermons by Marguerite Shuster (Grand Rapids, MI: William B. Eerdmans. 1996).

ELEVEN
MARKETPLACE PREACHING

Calvin Miller is a preacher, a poet, a painter, and one of Christianity's best loved writers. He currently serves as Professor of Preaching and Pastoral Ministry at Beeson Divinity School in Birmingham, Alabama. His books on preaching include Marketplace Preaching and The Empowered Communicator: 7 Keys to Unlocking an Audience.

DEREK MORRIS (DM): In your book *Marketplace Preaching*, you make a strong appeal for us to return the sermon to the marketplace.[1] What do you mean?

CALVIN MILLER (CM): I mean we should start with people where they are, not where we wish they were. The New Testament was written in Koine Greek, which was marketplace Greek. When it was translated into Latin by Jerome, it was put in vulgar or marketplace Latin. The marketplace is where people live and talk and where they say things in short sentences. Marketplace preaching keeps things in the vernacular. It's a line of conversation people can understand. It's what I call preaching in the vulgate. The church once again must learn to preach in the vulgate with marketplace sermons. Preachers must preach conversationally. They must appeal to those outside the church.

DM: So you want to bring the sermon back to where people can understand it.

CM: Yes. I have discovered that to grow a church from ten members to 3,500 members, you have to be able to start where the people are. Jesus Christ was a marketplace Savior. He was even criticized for being too marketplace. You see Jesus perching on the side of a well, trying to engage someone in conversation. The well was a center of activity, the marketplace, so to speak, and I think preaching needs to stay there.

DM: What is the most effective form for the marketplace sermon?

CM: I think story is a powerful form. I'm reading about the way lawyers are using stories. It is rare for a lawyer to present a case without saying, "Here is what happened," and the lawyer tells the jury a story. I read an article recently in the Wall Street Journal about lawyers using third-person stories to convince the jury certain things are true. Jesus used parables in the same way.

DM: How do you respond to those who suggest that expository preaching is more powerful than story, or narrative preaching?

CM: I say the story is the exposition. When Jesus was asked, "Who is my neighbor?" He didn't give a Hebrew root! He said, "A certain man went down to Jericho..." and told a story. Ten percent of the Bible is precept and 90 percent is narrative. I think for the marketplace mind, story is a powerful expositor.

DM: What is the best worship setting for the marketplace sermon?

CM: Marketplace preaching happens most effectively in the context of marketplace worship. "Vulgate worship," as I call it, must be relational, colloquial, and relevant. It must exist for and be understood by the person on the street. We can no longer build high, thick Gothic walls with colored glass to shut the world out. We must take the message into the world and preach it out in the open. One of the most impressive things Leif Anderson ever did was take his Easter services to the Mall of the Americas. Not a bad idea. That's where the world is passing by. People are passing through the mall, through the food court, not through the church. So you need to take your choir there and tell the story there. This is how Christianity began, and it flourished until they had buildings. Once we took on the provincialized view that we should separate ourselves from others and do our business away from the noise of the marketplace, we were much less effective and successful.

DM: You mention in *Marketplace Preaching* that the church seems more content to die inside than preach outside. Why do you think it is that way? Are we afraid to preach in the marketplace?

CM: Most of us feel a certain need to protect our testimony and our worship style. Christians are notorious for not wanting to talk about Jesus in the marketplace. They do that at church, but they won't at their job or the mall. We don't want anyone to be rude to us or to not like us for what we believe, so we think it's safer to not say anything in these settings. But if Christians would talk about Jesus in the marketplace, they would become more credible.

DM: What do you mean when you say effective marketplace preaching requires tight preparation and loose delivery?[2]

CM: One of the great appeals of story is spontaneity. When you hear Fred Craddock spin a yarn, it seems like he makes it up as he goes. But that isn't the case. There is tight preparation. I believe very much in writing out the sermon. I just don't think you can develop effective marketplace sermons without writing. I don't think you can produce anything that is going to be very enduring without writing it out. Whenever we finish preparing a sermon, we must go through it once more, sentence by sentence, replacing weak words with robust ones. Each of the sermon's key words must sing. Then phraseology has to be memorized. If you are going to use a line or two of a poem, memorize it. Go over everything in your mind until it's absolutely clear.

DM: I hear you saying the preparation must be tight, but what about the delivery of marketplace sermons?

CM: For the delivery, you need to hang loose, so if anything unexpected happens, you can laugh about it. On one occasion while a preacher was in the middle of the sermon, a little girl broke free, ran down the aisle, and came up onto the stage. The preacher stopped for a moment, picked her up, and said, "Isn't she beautiful?" The crowd broke into applause! Then the preacher said, "I don't know who she is, but you've got 30 seconds to claim her or she's mine!", and continued his sermon. This preacher spent a lot of time in his study, but he was hanging loose in his delivery. He appeared to be human, and humanity more than any other single horizontal quality sells a sermon.

The marketplace preacher has a genuine concern for the people who hear the message. This love for the people is even more important than a love for the subject. That's why I advocate "breaking" right before the sermon, which means for the last ten minutes before you preach, stop looking at the manuscript. Get away from it and meet a few people. Allow your hearers to become central. Get out of your document and into them. If you don't do that, you'll be riveted to your document, and you won't be able to identify with your hearers.

DM: Another strategy you suggest to connect with your hearers is the casual start, what you call the "speech before the speech."[3] What are you trying to accomplish in this casual start to the marketplace sermon?

CM: This is a relational age, but I don't think seminaries teach relational communication very well. They teach liturgy and high worship, but usually they don't touch on relational communication. When church planters go out to the storefront or the mall, they are talking to people who don't know liturgy. We have to start where people are. That's why relational communication is so important. Establishing a speaker-listener relationship is the main key to unlock effective communicating. Not much can happen until friendship is fixed. In the initial moments of building a listener relationship, the key has more to do with feeling than argument. Arguments are not heard until the emotive sense of speakers and listeners have merged. Only after we have reached an involved and relational oneness can we achieve a togetherness in our argument.

DM: I found myself chuckling when I read your marketplace strategies for maintaining the interest of your hearers. You suggest some radical tactics like the napalm file![4] Why is it so important for you to keep the attention of your audience?

CM: Nothing can happen once interest is gone. Nothing. People will not be inspired by what bores them. They have to be interested, and then they can be inspired. It hurts when I hear a preacher take a great truth and make it so boring that nobody cares. Interest is a key function in moving people from truth to inspiration and action.

DM: What counsel would you give to a pastor who senses the call to preach marketplace sermons?

CM: Analyze your audience. I take this pretty seriously. Usually, when I receive an invitation to preach, I ask: "Is your church formal or informal?" "How do you dress as a pastor?" "How do your people dress?" You don't want to violate that sense of who people are. When I preached for Will Willimon, I wore a robe, because everybody does. Rick Warren preaches without socks, but then people in his church in California go without socks.

Identity is a big issue, and if a preacher goes against that, the people feel distanced from him. So we need to identify with the audience. I also think a pastor's reading habits will determine his or her effectiveness in the marketplace. Read some best sellers, biographies, popular psychology. The more widely you can speak names that are authoritative to your audience, the more clout you will have.

And remember, a sermon is never done until the benediction is over. While you are preaching, it can be changed if it's not working. It can be added to, deleted, or even discarded. One morning, a man literally died of a heart attack in our worship service. I don't remember the sermon that day; what I remember is that as the rescue squad came to the church and into the sanctuary, I sat with his widow and prayed with her as the church joined around us in prayer. Those are moments when the preaching is of a totally different nature, but it is loud preaching. It is preaching where the people are: in the marketplace.

~

CHAPTER 11 — REFLECTION/DISCUSSION QUESTIONS

1. What aspect of marketplace preaching is most apparent in your sermons?

2. What are some ways you seek to connect with your hearers, both before you preach and while you are preaching?

3. What changes will you make to your preaching as a result of reading this chapter on marketplace preaching?

Notes:

1. "Marketplace Preaching." An interview with Calvin Miller, *Ministry* November 1998. Reprinted by permission.

2. Calvin Miller, *Marketplace Preaching: How to Return the Sermon to Where It Belongs* (Grand Rapids, MI: Baker Books, 1995), 96.

3. Calvin Miller, *The Empowered Communicator: 7 Keys to Unlocking an Audience* (Nashville, TN: Broadman and Holman, 1994), 19-24.

4. Ibid, 198,199.

TWELVE
CELEBRATION AND EXPERIENCE IN PREACHING

For over thirty years, Henry H. Mitchell has been recognized as an authority on Black preaching, and what he shares about preaching is relevant for preachers of any ethnic or cultural background. His preaching is known for its keen perception of what the Bible says here and now. His books include Black Preaching: The Recovery of a Powerful Art and Celebration and Experience in Preaching.

DEREK MORRIS (DM): Dr. Mitchell, you are a recognized authority on Black preaching.[1] Many have read your book *Black Preaching: The Recovery of a Powerful Art*.[2] What are some of the characteristics of Black preaching that make it such a powerful art?

HENRY H. MITCHELL (HM): Black preaching uses a medium of imagery and tonality to enhance the message. It isn't a downgrading of quality; it is an upgrading of effectiveness. Preaching has to be more than a cognitive essay, no matter how coherent, no matter how forceful the logic. People are not saved by logic; people are not saved by exciting, stimulating, intellectually impressive ideas; people are saved by faith, and faith is not an idea.

DM: Is that what you mean when you talk about needing to have an "experiential encounter" with the Word?[3]

HM: That's right! Faith is resident in intuition. It is not resident in cognition. If faith were resident in cognition, the smartest people would be the most likely to be saved. Nobody seems to understand that, but that's exactly the way it is. So if you put together a very impressive essay, you have impressed people, but there is no salvation in being impressed. People are ultimately saved by faith. Faith does not contradict reason in most cases. In fact, you need a certain amount of reason just to express faith. But ultimately people are prone to trust God on an intuitive basis.

DM: In *Celebration and Experience in Preaching,* you suggest sermons should be "designed to generate experiential encounter."[4] How does the preacher help people experience an encounter with the Word?

HM: If I want a person to experience something, I have to generate the kind of image with which they identify and therefore in which they participate vicariously. So when I paint a picture, I'm not just entertaining them. I'm providing a means whereby they can get on board this experience. When we come out at the end, the biblical story is their personal story. Whatever happened to the prodigal son happens to them.

DM: This idea of an image helping people make the Bible story their story reminds me of something you said in *The Recovery of Preaching:* "If you have an idea that can't be translated into a story or a picture, don't use it!"[5] Why is a story or a picture so important?

HM: An idea as idea is not self-evident. It's as simple as that. That's why Matthew, Mark and Luke seem to accuse Jesus of always using parables.

DM: The art of storytelling has a long history. Today narrative preaching is back in vogue but you point out that Black preaching has used narrative for generations.

HM: And I would hasten to suggest the narrative preaching talked about in so many western circles is still not what I'm talking about. The narrative preaching they're talking about focuses on cognitive goals. Explanation. While explanation is important, the bottom line is not how well the truth is explained but how high its impact is, and how much the Holy Spirit uses it to change people.

DM: So, the narrative is not simply a vehicle to convey information but a setting where listeners can experience an actual encounter with the Word. That's an important distinction. Let's look at another characteristic of Black preaching: dialogue. You assert that "proclamation with power requires dialogue."[6] Can you explain to us what is happening in the dialogue process?

HM: Participation occurs not only with responses like "Amen," but it occurs in the very attitude of people, because faith is more caught than taught. People who are deeply spiritual and deeply involved in the sermon tend to radiate a kind of influence that draws everybody else into it. It's like if you're at a funeral and see people crying, you have a hard time not crying. In a spiritually alive church, you'll hear a Black preacher say, "Somebody's not praying." Basically, what he is saying is, "I sense in this atmosphere a kind of coldness."

DM: Without congregational response, you maintain that "the sermon event would be impossible."[7] How does the preacher encourage the congregation to become more involved in dialogue?

HM: People need to be able to identify with what you're saying. You don't say, "Please say something" or "Please respond audibly." Quite the contrary. It ought to be something completely spontaneous. Audiences will participate to the extent they are drawn irresistibly into a powerful experience of encounter.

DM: Another characteristic of Black preaching you have identified is speaking in the mother tongue of your hearers. Can you explain what you mean by that?

HM: Language communicates a lot more than just the words. Language establishes identity in a powerful way. For instance, a man who is Black and speaks with a British accent will be heard and considered and received as British, no matter what his color. On the other hand, a man who is very light skinned and sounds like a brother will be perceived to be a brother. In other words, the ear image takes precedence over the eye image. No question about it. So if I'm talking to a group of young people and I speak with complete, proper, standard English, those young people will hear me as the enemy. But if I throw in a few of their words and make it plain to them that "I'm hip to what's happenin'," I'm in already. I don't care if I'm 90 years old. It's not a good thing to project a linguistic image that is false. But there is such a thing as becoming fluent in a variety of languages and doing what Paul recommended when he said, "I'm all things to all men." The point is, I identify with the audience by identifying with their language.

DM: So that's what you mean when you say a preacher needs to be "linguistically flexible."[8] You used the example of some great Black preachers who are very skilled with the language but will use some phrases of the mother tongue. Their intention is to create a more intimate connection with their hearers.

HM: Yes! You want people to identify with you. You want people to hear you. You want people to trust what you're saying. If they think of you as a stranger, they're not going to trust you. If, on the other hand, they think you have come from them or voluntarily joined them, then you have a ready audience.

DM: So, speaking in the mother tongue is a way to establish identity, to connect with your hearers. Obviously, that same principle can be applied in a variety of ethnic and cultural settings. Let's look at one other characteristic of Black preaching which is tremendously important: celebration. You not only assert that "expressive or emotional celebration should be understood as thoroughly biblical,"[9] you also insist that "celebration is a necessity"[10] and that "preaching without celebration is a de facto denial of the good news, in any culture."[11] What do you mean by celebration in preaching, and why is it so important?

HM: First of all, let's understand one thing: people are not going to do what the gospel says just because you said it's right. Ninety-nine times out of a hundred they already knew it was right, and they haven't done it. What makes you think just because you've said it, however cleverly, that they're suddenly going to change? People change when intuition and emotion unite with reason to alter behavior. In other words, there has to be a wholistic encounter.

Now, I'm going to involve emotion. I have to do it in a purposeful way. It isn't just excitement. A lot of people think the celebrated end of a Black sermon is just for entertainment purposes. People aren't changed until their feelings are changed. If you can emote with focus, emote purposefully, you'll have an audience that goes away wanting to do what the Word says because the whole person has been impacted. So I celebrate knowing that if people are impacted by my celebration they're much more likely to do what they're supposed to do.

DM: Even though you suggest that "it will not be easy to begin to design vicarious experiences and celebrations of the Word"[12] you obviously believe it is both possible and important for any preacher who wishes to communicate God's Word effectively.

HM: It's not all that hard if you follow the rules. First, in order to celebrate you move out of the cognitive mode. You don't just conclude with a cognitive summary but you find a way to be glad, a very simple way to be glad about the truth contained in the sermon. If you get glad about it, you want to do it.

Second, you can't celebrate what's wrong. You've got to have a positive text and a basically positive sermon. You celebrate because the prodigal son came home. That's what gladness is about. It's the good news. This gladness transforms people in a way that a critical comment never would. Indeed, if you actually succeeded through critical comment in giving people a bad conscience, you would only be succeeding in giving what a psychiatrist would call a guilt neurosis. People are not saved by guilt neurosis. A sermon has to start positively, and it has to end positively.

Third, don't introduce new information in the celebration. This is not because people are dumb; it's because they already have the truth, and now you're just putting that last blow of the hammer to drive it all the way in. It's the ecstatic reinforcement of the Word. Now we use heightened rhetoric and beauty of phrase to touch people, things we would not use in the earlier more conscious moves in the sermon.

Fourth, the preacher has to be caught up in celebration. You can't expect people to be glad about something if you're not glad. If you're so chained to a manuscript that you can't really rejoice, that you can't be transparently a part of the words you're preaching, you've got a problem. The preacher helps the people to catch the spirit. If you have any logical reason to expect the Lord to work, you ought to be involved in it yourself. We are celebrating the behavioral purposes of the sermon. We're celebrating the truth. We're not just up there dancing around. We are giving what I call ecstatic reinforcement to the text, and until you've had that ecstatic reinforcement, the whole person has not yet met the text.

DM: As preachers lead congregations in an experience of celebration, what safeguards them against going to emotional excess?

HM: There is no such thing as excess, if you go at it properly. In the first place, you do what you can, and the Holy Spirit does the rest. In the second place, this celebration is intentional emotion, focused emotion, and if it's focused, there is no way it's going to excess. There are a lot of people who end up throwing away the baby with the bath water when they fear that almost any emotional expression is going to lead them out of control. They are so busy being proper, they forget that the Holy Ghost has got good sense. And if it's really a Holy Ghost motivated celebration, there's nothing that's going to get out of hand. If preachers go beyond the Holy Spirit, they're on their own. That's manipulation. That's not authentic celebration.

~

CHAPTER 12 — REFLECTION/DISCUSSION QUESTIONS

1. How has your cultural heritage enhanced or hampered your preaching?

2. What characteristics of Black preaching resonate with you?

3. How do you respond to Mitchell's assertion that celebration in preaching is a necessity?

Notes:

1. "Celebration and Experience in Preaching." An interview with Henry H. Mitchell, *Ministry* March 2001. Reprinted by permission.

2. Henry H. Mitchell, *Black Preaching: The Recovery of a Powerful Art* (Nashville, TN: Abingdon Press, 1990).

3. Henry H. Mitchell, *Celebration and Experience in Preaching* (Nashville, TN: Abingdon Press, 1990), 25.

4. Ibid., 139.

5. Mitchell, *The Recovery of Preaching* (San Francisco, CA: Harper & Row, 1977), 45.

6. Ibid., 115.

7. *Black Preaching: The Recovery of a Powerful Art,* 1 13.

8. Ibid., 87.

9. *Celebration and Experience in Preaching,* 26.

10. *Black Preaching,* 131.

11. *The Recovery of Preaching,* 54.

12. *Celebration and Experience in Preaching,* 139.

THIRTEEN
PREACHING THAT TURNS THE WORLD UPSIDE DOWN

William H. Willimon is Bishop of the North Alabama Conference of the United Methodist Church and former Dean of the Chapel at Duke University. He is author of numerous books and articles on preaching and has been recognized as one of the top twelve "most effective preachers in the English-speaking world."

DEREK MORRIS (DM): I would like to begin with the glorious accusation in the book of Acts, brought against Paul and Silas, which says that these Christian preachers had "turned the world upside down" (Acts 17:6).[1] What can we learn about preaching from this experience?

WILLIAM H. WILLIMON (WW): The book of Acts has a paradigm for our work. In Acts, Christian missionaries move into the world, telling the story of Christ. Each time it's told, it has a little different emphasis, but it's still the same story. Sometimes the world responds positively, as in Acts 2, but many times, the response is nothing but a beating and a trip to jail. When you say "Jesus Christ is Lord," it tends to throw other lords into disarray. It did with Herod when Jesus was born, and it does with Caesar in Acts. The result is opposition and rejection. The thing I love in the Acts drama is that the Christian missionaries don't care. They'd love to have their preaching accepted, but they tell their story regardless. For every story of evangelistic success, Luke usually follows with stories of failure.

DM: So preaching that turns the world upside down doesn't inevitably lead to success as people count success. There may be baptisms in one setting and beatings in the other.

WW: That's right. In Acts, they seem more worried about getting the story right than anything else. You don't know whether Luke is more excited about being rejected or being accepted. He loves to tell a story of success: Peter came out, said just a few words to them, they were pricked to the heart, and asked "What can we do to be saved?" Luke loves to tell of the thousands who were saved, but he also tells that these preachers were willing to suffer rejection. In fact, I think it's a discredit to my preaching that I don't preach the gospel well enough to get more rejection.

DM: We don't hear that honest warning very often. But the record is clear: Preaching that turned the world upside down has some rather unpredictable results. In the book *Preaching to Strangers,* which you co-authored with Stanley Hauerwas, you warned that "Christian conversation with strangers can be dangerous."[2] What other dangers does the preacher face, besides rejection?

WW: In attempting to speak to the world as Christ commands us to, sometimes we fall into the world, face down. The world gets us. Jesus tells us to go out and get the world. Then He tells us, "You be careful; they're out to get you!" One danger I face when preaching to strangers is that in my earnest efforts to spread the gospel, I end up offering less than the gospel. Or I try to crank the gospel down to something that anybody staggering off the street can get in five minutes. Or I try to say, "Let's see, are you interested in self-esteem? Well, salvation is something like that." Or, "Would you like to feel better about yourself? Well, Jesus can help you." I think we need to keep being reminded of how odd it is that we preach Jesus Christ and Him crucified. The world has lots of ways of reminding us: "Hey, you people are kind of on the fringe of what success looks like." That's a good thing.

DM: I hear you saying that preaching that turns the world upside down is not simply a restatement of the popular gospel of the culture. We need to boldly proclaim the gospel of Jesus Christ, even when it may seem odd or strange to others.[3] Can you give us an example?

WW: Yes, there's one in Acts 17. This passage is sometimes used as a great example of Paul getting "down and dirty" with the Athenians. He quotes from some of their poets. He talks about this altar to an unknown God. Then, as he ends his sermon, he says, "This god that you grope for, I proclaim to you as the One whom God has raised from the dead, and the One who shall come and judge everybody." This gets the Athenians scoffing. There may be a lot of evidence out there that nature is beautiful and orderly, like the snowflake, but there isn't any evidence out there for the resurrection. At the end of that sermon in Athens, some of Paul's hearers say, "That's the stupidest thing we've ever heard!" Only a few are converted, including Dionysius the Areopagite and a woman named Damaris. Pretty small pickings for one of the greatest speeches in the New Testament.

DM: In your book, *The Intrusive Word*, you suggest, when preaching to the un-converted, "our preaching ought to be so confrontational...that it requires no less than a miracle to be heard."[4] How can preachers be confrontational without being offensive?

WW: When we confront people, we're doing so in the name of the Prince of Peace, the Slain Lamb. As Christians, we don't have any means of working other than with words. We're not allowed to pull the sword on somebody and tell them to be converted. The only thing we've got is the foolishness of preaching. Words can be powerful, even if they present a different kind of power. I remember someone telling me she was offended by my sermon. I said, "I was too." She said, "Really? I thought you liked it," and I said, "We don't preach this stuff because we like it. We preach it because we've been told to preach it." Christianity confronts every cul-ture, including the first culture in which it found itself. We should not be surprised when our Christian description of what's going on in the world clashes with the culture's understanding of what's happening. The world doesn't know it's terminal. The world thinks it's invulnerable and eternal. The world thinks we can keep going upward and onward.

Years ago, I was in a campus discussion on nuclear arms. One group said, "We're going to blow ourselves to bits. We're sitting on a nuclear keg, and the fuse is lit. We're going to blow away life as we know it." The other group said, "No, the Rus-sians have got the bomb; we need the bomb. We're defending life as we know it, and the best way to do that is let them know we're not going to use our bomb if they're not going to use their bomb." I said, "You know, it's nice that both of you agree that the issue is surviving and the mutual question is how best to survive, but as Christians, we don't think we're going to survive. We actually believe God is not linked to the American way or any particular way. God has no great investment in whether the world as we know it lasts for a thousand years, or not."

DM: You suggest that "preaching becomes invigorated when...Jesus gets loose again, and people come out of the service stunned."[5] What does that look like?

WW: Once I did a retreat for students who had heard of Jesus but were not yet ready to follow Him. About a dozen people attended. I did all kinds of things. The first night I showed them the Gospel of Mark, done by an actor who just recited it straight. When we were through, this guy with long hair and tears in his eyes said, "Boy, Jesus is cool. I knew right from the beginning that they were going to kill Him. I mean, I just knew it." I said, "Really?" He replied, "You know, I understand why they killed Him, because you just can't go around saying stuff like that without people wanting to kill you." There, in a certain wonderful moment, Jesus broke loose. When someone says he can't sleep at night and he feels guilty over his behavior, I just sit there in awe. It's amazing that God can get through, because we've got such wonderful defenses against God. I just give God the glory when those defenses crumble.

DM: That's powerful! Where do you find the courage to keep delivering God's outrageous truths to people? You mentioned that you haven't been beaten recently, but people may beat you verbally or respond with scoffing or patronizing disinterest. Where do you find the courage to continue to preach in a way that turns people upside down?

WW: I have to admit, I'm very well protected. I'm in a bishop appointed system, you know. I was talking to a group of Southern Baptist pastors about courage in the pulpit. Three hundred Southern Baptist pastors get fired every month. It takes courage to speak up. Walter Brueggemann suggests that if you're a coward by nature, that's OK. God can still use you because what you can still do is get down behind the text! Just get down behind it and push it out there in front of the people. You can still say something like this: "Can you believe God said *that* to us? What does God want out of us now? You're the ones who showed up here in church today and said you wanted to hear God's Word, so here it is!" Then the preacher can make a bold application and say, "This is not necessarily what I'm saying, but I believe this is what the text is saying." I love that! But courage is also found in the text itself. A lot of times when people come and criticize something I've said, I sit there and say, "Lord, I can't believe You've done that to me. I mean, I'm the most compromised, cowardly person in the world, but You've actually made me courageous for 20 minutes. That is a miracle! Thank You. I can't believe You did that!" When God turns the world upside down through preaching, it's not a disaster; it is an act of grace.

~

CHAPTER 13 — REFLECTION/DISCUSSION QUESTIONS

1. How would your congregation describe your sermons?

2. What is the difference between bold preaching and offensive preaching?

3. How has your preaching changed through the years and why have those changes occurred?

Notes:

1. "Preaching that Turns the World Upside Down." An interview with William H. Willimon, *Ministry* November 1999. Reprinted by permission.

2. William H. Willimon and Stanley Hauerwas, *Preaching to Strangers: Evangelism in Today's World* (Louisville, KY: Westminster/John Knox Press), 139.

3. For an excellent discussion on this topic, read the chapter entitled "Preaching to Pagans" in William H. Willimon, *Peculiar Speech: Preaching to the Baptized* (Grand Rapids, MI: William B. Eerdmans, 1992), 75-94.

4. William H. Willimon, *The Intrusive Word: Preaching to the Unbaptized* (Grand Rapids, MI: William B. Eerdmans, 1994), 22.

5. Marshall Shelley and Jim Berkley, "Pumping Truth to a Disinclined World," Leadership (Spring 1990): 131.

FOURTEEN
EMBRACING THE NEXT GENERATION

Josh McDowell is an internationally known Christian speaker and author. He has spoken to more than 7 million young people in 84 countries, including visits to 700 university and college campuses. He has authored or co-authored more than 75 books that have sold more than 10 million copies. Among his most popular books are Beyond Belief to Convictions, The New Evidence That Demands a Verdict, and More Than a Carpenter.[1]

DEREK MORRIS (DM): As a Christian apologist and evangelist, you have probably spoken to as many young people about Jesus Christ as any in the history of the Christian church.[1] Share with us one of your most memorable experiences.

JOSH MCDOWELL (JM): I was in Phoenix, doing a high school assembly. On the first day, there were about fifteen hundred students outside at noon. I stood on a huge boulder in order to connect more effectively with the crowd. I had been warned that there was a group of Gothics on campus who would try to break up the assembly. I had just started to speak when six Gothics came up and stood about ten feet away from me. They were dressed in black, with tattoos and piercings on every part of their bodies. They just stood there and scowled at me. Without the crowd knowing it, I changed my topic and spoke about intimacy. I shared that Christ can give you the capacity to be real with another person. When my talk was over, I stepped off the boulder and the head of the Gothics leaped toward me. The whole crowd gasped. He came within six inches of my face. There were tears running down his cheeks. He said to me very respectfully, "Mr. McDowell, would you give me a hug?" And before I could even say "Yes," this young man put his head on my shoulder and cried like a baby. Then he said to me, "My father never once hugged me or told me he loved me."

That story keeps coming back to me whenever I stand up to speak. Young people need to know God loves them, and who are His instruments to share His love? We are.

DM: When did you first discover a passion to tell young people about Jesus Christ and God's amazing love?

JM: After I committed my life to Jesus Christ in my late teens, I immediately wanted to tell the whole world about Him. I was born running! I have a passion for young people because that's where I was when I came to know Christ. I started out my Christian ministry talking to university students. I have spoken on over seven hundred university and college campuses. But a major shift occurred 15 years ago. I realized that decisions once made in university were now being made in eighth, ninth, and tenth grades. So now I focus my ministry on 12 to 17-year-olds. I want to reach kids for Christ before they have made a lot of decisions that are going to negatively affect them for the rest of their lives. After about 13 years of age in today's culture, a young person is hardened like young people were after university 15 years ago. Young people are being confronted with different world-views and conflicting ideas at a younger age. For example, 15 years ago Islam was a religion in a different part of the world. Now it's next door. Today, with free access to the Internet, anything you believe as a Christian is challenged. That wasn't true 15 years ago. That's why George Barna suggests from his research that if you don't reach young people in today's culture by age 13, you might never reach them.

DM: You've been involved in ministry to young people for over 40 years. What keeps you going?

JM: One reason why I keep on reaching out to young people for Christ is that I am so grateful for my own salvation. I'm overwhelmed that the Creator God of the universe wants a relationship with me. In Exodus 34:14, He says "I am passionate about my relationship with you." I'm just overwhelmed with that! So, every time I see someone, especially a young person, that verse pops into my mind. God wants a relationship with that person! He wants pastors, youth pastors, and parents to be the channel for establishing that relationship with God.

A second reason why I keep reaching out to young people for Christ is because I believe that every person's destiny is dependent on how they relate to Jesus Christ. I am more convinced than ever that Jesus Christ is the Messiah, the Son of God. So, young people need to hear the truth about Jesus Christ.

Thirdly, I keep on reaching out to young people for Christ because there are so many hurting kids in the world today. There is one word to describe today's mosaic generation: Abandoned. Young people feel abandoned emotionally and spiritually. They need to experience God's love.

DM: You mention on your Web site www.beyondbelief.com that we need a spiritual revolution in the Christian community—a CrossCulture revolution.[3] What do you mean by that?

JM: I hate to say this, but right now we are losing the battle. We are not seeing transformation in the lives of professed Christian young people. Seventy-five to eighty percent of our young people are leaving the church. Research by Barna, Gallup, and others shows there is hardly any difference between a young person inside the church and a secular young person outside the church. It used to be that on issues like lying, stealing, or cheating, there was a 14 to 18 percent difference between professed Christians and unbelievers. Now, it's less than three percent difference. We are beyond needing a reformation. We need a revolution, a drastic change.

DM: What are some ways we can be more intentional in reaching young people for Jesus Christ?

JM: Providing a loving environment is one way you can be more intentional in reaching young people for Christ. Young people need a loving environment in order to flourish. Ideally, a young person needs a Christian home, where Mom and

Dad are in love with each other and love their kids, and their kids sense that love. Research sponsored by the YMCA, Dartmouth Medical School, and the Institute for American Values showed that young people are hardwired for enduring connections to others and for moral and spiritual meaning.[4]

Secondly, if you want to be more intentional in reaching young people for Jesus Christ and passing on your values to the next generation, you must live out that truth in their presence. Teach your children, or the young people within your circle of influence, not only the "what's" but the "why's" of the faith. When that happens, it is very likely the young person will assimilate the Christian faith.

Over the years, my wife and I have watched many movies with our kids. On 20 to 25 occasions, we got up and walked out of the theater. That had an impact on our kids. Now we'll hear our kids say, "We went to watch a movie with some friends last night, but we got up and left!" Where did they find the courage to walk out? I had modeled for them the importance of being careful what you take into your mind, and the courage to walk out if necessary.

Thirdly, if you want to be more intentional in reaching young people for Christ, model what it looks like to share your faith. Be actively involved in changing the world. Talk about missions. Be involved in the community. Look for people, for events, for seminars, for conferences that will supplement what you are teaching and modeling to your children. Go on mission trips. Each year, ask yourself, "What seminars do we want our kids to attend this year?"

DM: As you view the Christian church as a whole, what obstacles or barriers are preventing young people from finding a personal relationship with Jesus Christ?

JM: One obstacle is this: Young people are not seeing dynamic, living, examples of Christ's life within the body of Christ. A young African-American woman, Lena Williams, put it this way: "We are not seeing God's love through other people." When today's generation sees a lack of authentic modeling, they say, "It's not true." Biblically, all truth is taught in the context of relationships. Young people are looking for truth that works. If they don't see it working in their own lives, they will say, "It's not true." This is why it is so important for us to live our faith in the presence of our children.

DM: I was impressed by your answer to a young person on your Web site who was struggling with impure thoughts and actions. Like many committed Christians, both young and old, she wanted to honor Jesus Christ by maintaining pure thoughts and actions, but it was a struggle for her. You spoke about pure thoughts displacing impure thoughts, and about the importance of memorizing Scripture.

JM: In the flesh, you will never resist impure thoughts and actions. We need to teach our children to be filled with the Holy Spirit by faith. It is the indwelling presence of God's Spirit that strengthens us. It's a simple process: Desire to be filled, because the Bible says, "Blessed are those who hunger and thirst for righteousness, for they shall be filled" (Matt. 5:6). Have no unconfessed sin in your life. The Bible says, "If we confess our sins, He is faithful and just to forgive us our sins and to cleanse us from all unrighteousness" (1 John 1:9). And then, ask the Holy Spirit to fill you. "If we ask anything according to His will, He hears us. And if we know that He hears us, whatever we ask, we know that we have the petitions that we have asked of Him" (1 John 5:14,15).

Once we have asked to be filled with the Holy Spirit, we need to recognize that God uses His Word to transform us. Only as we put Scripture into our hearts and minds can it replace those thoughts which can be so destructive. You can cooperate with the Holy Spirit in the process of renewing your mind by striving to replace impure thoughts with pure thoughts. When you pour liquid into a test tube, it forces the gas out. In the same way, pure thoughts can force impure thoughts out of your mind. Memorizing and meditating on Scripture is particularly helpful. Here are some useful tips to help you memorize Scripture: Decide to memorize at least one verse per week. Start with these: Romans 12:1, 2; Psalm 51:10; Colossians 3:1-3; and Philippians 4:8. Memorize word for word. Don't make up your own translation. Think about the verse. Ask what this verse means and what God is saying to you through this verse. Apply the verse to your life. "As a result of this verse, I will _____." Review. Go over the new verse every day for two months. Then once a week after that. The psalmist said that he hid God's Word in his heart to help keep him from sin (Ps. 119:11). When you ask to be filled with the Holy Spirit and fill your mind with the Word of God, you will be blessed!

DM: What are some resources that can help us reach young people for Christ?

JM: There is Dare 2 Share with Greg Stier.[5] They have a vision to train one million teens to clearly and confidently share their faith and to establish thirty thousand evangelism teams (e-teams) nationwide. It's a marvelous movement, and they are reaching thousands of kids for Christ. WisdomWords Ministries, with Mark Matlock, holds PlanetWisdom conferences to help young people grow into a deeper personal relationship with Jesus Christ.[6] I thank God for Mark. Then there's Teen Mania with Ron Luce.[7] There is nowhere you can go where your faith will become more contagious than Teen Mania. Ron challenges teenagers to take a stand for Christ in their schools, communities, and throughout the world. Paul Fleischmann and the National Network of Youth Ministries are working with over eight thousand youth pastors. Their goal is to expose every teenager to the gospel of Jesus Christ.[8] Youth Specialties works alongside Christian youth workers of just about every denomination and youth-serving organization.[9] They are providing resources and training for thousands of youth pastors every year. And then there is our own ministry, Beyond Belief.[10] We are committed to equipping young people in this generation to become so thoroughly convinced of the reality and relevance of Jesus Christ and His Word that they act on their Christian convictions regardless of the consequences.

There are so many resources. The structure is there, the foundation is there, but we still have a great work to do to reach the next generation for Christ. We need to pray, be faithful to our commission as the body of Christ, and God the Holy Spirit will move!

~

CHAPTER 14 — REFLECTION/DISCUSSION QUESTIONS

1. Josh McDowell suggests we are losing the battle with young people in our churches. How would you respond to that assertion as you consider your community?

2. Who has inspired you as an effective Christian communicator to young people?

3. How will your preaching ministry to young people change as a result of reading this chapter?

Notes:

1. www.josh.org.

2. "Embracing the Next Generation." An interview with Josh McDowell, *Ministry* March 2006. Reprinted by permission.

3. www.beyondbelief.com.

4. www.americanvalues.org/html/hardwired.html.

5. www.dare2share.org.

6. www.planetwisdom.org.

7. www.teenmania.org.

8. www.youthworkers.net.

9. www.youthspecialities.com.

10. www.beyondbelief.com.

FIFTEEN
EVANGELISTIC PREACHING

Charles D. Brooks has preached the Word of God for more than half a century. As a result of his evangelistic preaching, thousands have accepted Christ as their personal Savior. For 23 years, he served as director-speaker of the Breath of Life television ministry.

DEREK MORRIS (DM): For more than fifty years, you have preached the Word of God with holy boldness.[1] Just like Timothy, you have done "the work of an evangelist" (2 Tim. 4:2, 5). Through your ministry God has touched thousands of lives. When did you first hear the call to preach?

CHARLES D. BROOKS (CB): I had no intention of becoming a preacher. I had already been accepted into a predentistry program, and two weeks before classes began the Lord spoke to me. I was sitting in Earl Cleveland's evangelistic tent, by myself, and the Lord impressed my mind in a most definite way: "This is what I want you to do, and I will help you to make truth clear." I spoke to my mother about this. She said to me, "Son, when you were born, I gave you to the Lord. Now, He's calling you." And I have never looked back.

DM: When I was a young preacher in Pennsylvania, I listened to your evangelistic sermons. I had never heard anyone preach the Word with such boldness. It was as if you had fire in your bones! Is evangelism a special gift or is every preacher called to preach evangelistic sermons?

CB: I believe there is the special gift of "evangelist." That is not something I chose. But I also believe everyone who is called to preach is called to preach the truth of God's Word.

DM: I have noticed many young preachers are skeptical about evangelistic preaching. They have been told the days of public evangelistic preaching are over. Some are convinced people won't come to a public meeting and listen to someone preach. How would you respond to that skepticism?

CB: This idea that it won't work didn't come from God. The best days of evangelism are before us. We are going to see thousands baptized in a day. And it's happening now. I was holding some meetings in Chicago, and about fifteen young preachers were assigned to work with me. Some of them were skeptical about evangelistic preaching. But those young preachers worked with us, and more than two hundred individuals committed their lives to Christ and were baptized! Those young preachers found a passion for evangelistic preaching.

DM: I've noticed in your evangelistic sermons that you challenge your hearers to think. Here's an excerpt from one of your sermons on the theme of salvation: "Our subject tonight deals with a question that is so vital, I don't know how to impress you with its importance. Friends, please do this, for your own sake. When you came in you were given a blank piece of paper. We wish you'd use that piece of paper to write down the Scriptures we give you, and any notes you might like to take. You're going to hear things from night to night as you continue attending that you perhaps have not heard before, and you need to check to see if I'm telling you the truth. Do you know, one of the reasons there's so much confusion in the Christian church today is folks just sit and swallow everything that preachers say. Now you don't know me. So check and see if it's there. And if it's not there, you don't have to believe it."[2]

That's a refreshing approach. You challenge your hearers to think with you. Did you learn that approach from other evangelists or did you develop that style as a result of personal experience?

CB: To be honest with you, I don't think I've given five minutes thought to style. This is just the way my mind is influenced to work. I was taught that because truth is offensive to unbelievers, we have to be wise in presenting it. I will often present a proposition that demands scriptural proof. I believe there is power in the Word.

There was a mother in Columbus, Ohio, who picked up one of my handbills and began reading the topics. She then called her daughter and said, "Let's go and see what this fool is talking about!" They came to the meeting, and while I was preaching the sermon, I saw a whole row of people stand. As they stood, I thought, Lord, have I offended these people? Are they walking out? But instead of walking out, they turned and started walking to the front. When they got closer, I saw it was this mother, her daughter, and their children. No appeal had been made. There's power in the Word of God!

DM: Evangelistic preaching involves calling people to make life-changing decisions. That's intimidating to some preachers. What counsel would you give to preachers about calling for a response as part of evangelistic preaching?

CB: I've had some preachers tell me they become so nervous when they call people to respond to the Word of God that they are actually falling apart! I would say to them, "When you feel that you are responsible for how people will respond, you are actually taking on a responsibility that is not yours."

Our responsibility as preachers is to give our hearers an opportunity to respond. What happens in the heart of the hearer is between that person and God. If you give an invitation for people to accept Christ and no one responds, don't feel bad. Maybe everyone is saved already! Don't be afraid to give an invitation.

DM: Can you give us an example of an invitation you might give for people to accept Christ as their personal Savior?

CB: I might say something like this: "Jesus has gone to prepare a place for you in the heavenly city. Some day soon He's coming to take you home, and the gates of that city are going to swing open. The saints are going to go marching in. Ladies and gentlemen, who are these people? They are rotten, no-good sinners who are redeemed by the blood of the Lamb. We're going to glory to be with Jesus. That's what lies just ahead, and it's ours by faith, because Christ has opened the way. I want to be saved. I want to go to that place where the tree of life is blooming, where there is rest for the weary.

"Somewhere in the fields of Eden God's people can get together. I want to see you there. I want you to see me. I want to shake your hand in the kingdom. Most of all, Jesus wants to see you there. Jesus died that you might be there. He shed His precious blood that you might be saved, that your sins might be washed away and that you might have power to live for Him.

"My question tonight is, How many of you want to accept what Jesus has done for you and want to be saved in His kingdom? If you do, I want you all to stand with me right now as we pray."

Here is another example: "It's decision time. It's time for full surrender. It's time to let Christ take those wrong desires and make something new out of you. If you want to let some things go now, and have your life converted so you don't even miss them, if you want to stand at the foot of the cross this morning and fully surrender your life to Jesus, I want you to stand up right now as we talk to the Lord."

DM: Your examples remind me of an invitation at the conclusion of a sermon by Billy Graham titled "Conversion." He concluded his sermon with these words: "I tell you, when you come to Christ, I do not care when it is, I do not care where it is, how it is when you come, you will have to come by repentance and faith, trusting in Him and His death and resurrection alone for salvation. If you haven't come, if you haven't met Christ there, I am asking you to do it tonight. You may be a member of the church. You may be a choir member. You may be an usher here. You may be a Sunday School teacher. But you are not sure that you have actually met Christ and been converted. You want to be sure, and you want to settle it. I am going to ask you to get up out of your seat and come here and say, 'Tonight I will receive Him. I will repent. I will give my life to Christ.'"[3]

CB: That's a good example of a simple invitation. As you listen to evangelistic sermons, you learn there are many ways to give an invitation. Billy Graham used to say, "I'm just going to stand here. You come." The goal is more than merely an emotional response. I tell people, "I want you to think. I would rather you think than just shout and become excited."

DM: When you invite people to respond, I have noticed you aren't just reciting words off a piece of paper. Your words, intonation, and body language communicate a heartfelt concern for your hearers.

CB: That's important! People can tell if you are real. I remember the first time I did extensive evangelistic preaching with an interpreter. I was in Egypt. I got a note one night written in Arabic, and I asked the interpreter to translate it. It said, "Dear Pastor, We listen to him, but we watch you! And we can tell by your eyes that you mean what you say." I've never forgotten that. I don't preach anything that I don't believe. I don't preach anything that I can't preach with conviction. People can see it. They can feel it. They know if you're just up there doing a job. I want people to feel that I am under the control of the Holy Spirit, and they are too. And it's never to me that they respond. It's to Him.

DM: I hear you saying it is vitally important to really believe what you are preaching. Your hearers can tell if you are genuine or not. Is there any other counsel you would give to a preacher who senses God's call to preach to lost people?

CB: There is the danger of wanting to come across as extremely erudite. But the Bible says Jesus talked to common people, and they heard Him gladly. Read all you want. Fill your head. But when you preach, be simple, honest, direct. People will absorb the message better. They will feel more at ease with you. Don't try to impress your hearers. Be interested in them, and love them.

When you're preaching, effective eye contact is extremely important. I like to look at people and see how they are being affected. And always remember you are simply a messenger. Nothing of self is to be projected. People are not to be won to you.

DM: What word of encouragement would you give to preachers who sense the call to preach evangelistic sermons?

CB: When you preach evangelistic sermons, you are doing what God called you to do! God doesn't call you to entertain. He doesn't call you to be witty. God calls you to preach the Word. So make sure you know the Word yourself, and when you preach the Word, it's going to have an effect!

~

CHAPTER 15 — REFLECTION/DISCUSSION QUESTIONS

1. What are your thoughts and feelings when you hear the term *evangelistic preaching*?

2. Reflect on the times you have called people to respond to the preaching of the Word of God. What lessons have you learned?

3. How will your approach to evangelistic preaching change as a result of reading this chapter?

Notes:
1. "Preaching the Word." An interview with evangelist Charles D. Brooks, *Ministry* April 2005. Reprinted by permission.
2. From an audio recording of the sermon "Claimed and Kept" by Charles D. Brooks.
3. Billy Graham at the Charlotte, North Carolina evangelistic crusade in 1958, <http://www.wheaton.edu/bgc/archives/docs/bg-charlotte/1003.html>.

SIXTEEN
PROPHETIC PREACHING

Hyveth Williams is Professor of Homiletics at the Seventh-day Adventist Theological Seminary, Andrews University, Berrien Springs, Michigan.

DEREK MORRIS (DM): In recent years there has been a growing interest in prophetic preaching.[1] Let's start with a definition.

HYVETH WILLIAMS (HW): Prophetic preaching is a biblically based form of proclamation in which the preacher exercises the divine authority to be a spokesperson for God. When I speak of authority, I mean that which Jesus had. It caused the crowds to be amazed at His teaching for He was teaching them as one having authority, and not as their scribes (see Matt. 7:28, 29). While power is a natural derivative of authority, exercising it out of self-will is always dangerous and oppressive. But when power comes from the divine gift of authority, it becomes liberating and redemptive.

DM: Isn't that what is supposed to happen in all anointed biblical preaching? What makes prophetic preaching unique?

HW: Yes, all biblical preachers are to exercise this authority, but prophetic preaching speaks up for God's justice in a way that is different and relevant to the needs or plight of hearers. Prophetic preaching critically challenges the status quo. Prophetic preachers are not preoccupied with being politically correct. Unlike so-called "patriot pastors,"[2] prophetic preachers are willing to confront injustice in the nation as well as in their local communities with divine authority. Jesus gave that authority to His disciples (Luke 9:1, 2). Listeners can identify this authority in the delivery of messages because the messenger displays the holy boldness of a lion's heart empowered by the Holy Spirit. I take my cue to preach prophetically from Ellen White who addressed the controversial issue of racism in a powerful prophetic sermon delivered on March 21, 1891, to a group of General Conference leaders.

DM: Can you share something with us from that sermon?

HW: Of course. She said: "There has been much perplexity as to how our laborers in the South shall deal with the 'color line.' It has been a question to some how far to concede to the prevailing prejudice against the colored people. The Lord has given us light concerning all such matters. There are principles laid down in His Word that should guide us in dealing with these perplexing questions. The Lord Jesus came to our world to save men and women of all nationalities. He died just as much for the colored people as for the white race."[3] Believe me, she rankled the brethren and paid a price for her forthrightness.

DM: That is what Leonora Tubbs Tisdale talks about in her book *Prophetic Preaching: A Pastoral Approach,* when she says, "Prophetic preaching is counter-cultural and challenges the status quo."[4]

HW: Exactly. Prophetic preaching not only challenges the status quo but offers theological and biblical insights into the current human situation from an individual's enslavement to sin to current cries for freedom echoed around the world in massive protests. It provides divinely orchestrated strategies on how to move out of despair with determination and hope.

DM: Tisdale also asserts that "Prophetic preaching is concerned with the evils and shortcomings of the present social order and is often more focused on corporate and public issues than on individual and personal concerns."[5] So how does prophetic preaching connect with the life of the individual hearer and not simply address broad social concerns?

HW: Corporate sin is intimately connected to personal transgression. In fact, corporate sin begins in the head of an individual long before it gets into the system to pollute or pervert it. That's why it's important to confront individual sin before it becomes the root of corporate evil. For example, there's a definite connection between adultery and corporate corruption because a person who is unfaithful to a spouse will more likely be deceptive in their dealings in the marketplace. Prophetic preachers need to speak clearly and powerfully about where we have gone wrong, personally, and then show how to get back on track with God both individually and corporately.

DM: Share with us some specific steps in the preparation of a prophetic sermon.

HW: The first step is to study and integrate the Word of God into one's mind and soul. This precedes any specific sermon preparation because the prophetic preacher must speak of a God who is known personally to them and can be loved by all. Recently, I was studying the passage in 2 Timothy 2:15 where the apostle Paul encourages the young preacher Timothy to "be diligent to present yourself approved to God, a worker who does not need to be ashamed, rightly dividing the word of truth." The Greek word spoudazo (diligent), also translated as "study," means "to be very active," implying more than being acquainted with information but possessing the noble trait which distinguishes productive servants of God.

DM: So the first step is to be filled with the Word of God, not just theoretically but in an active life-changing way. What's the second step in prophetic preaching?

HW: The prophetic preacher needs to carefully examine the present cultural, social, or religious situation and then put that situation into a theological and biblical perspective. This is accomplished by asking some pertinent questions: Where have the people gone wrong? How have they turned away from God's ideal? What role did their leaders play in this error? In 2006, Dr. Calvin Butts, of Abyssinian Baptist Church in New York,[6] preached a sermon at Oakwood University entitled "Of

Towers and Lights."[7] He compared the falling of the Twin Towers of the World Trade Center in New York City to the story of the Tower of Babel in Genesis 11. He showed how the activity of leaders had destroyed honor and diminished beauty. He noted that the language of the financial community had become confused. Then he spoke a word from the Lord, calling people to reinstate the language of holiness in all their activities. That sermon was a wonderful example of prophetic preaching.

DM: So prophetic preaching goes beyond simply pointing out what is wrong either with the social order or in individual lives. Tisdale notes, "Prophetic preaching requires the preacher to name both what is not of God in the world (criticizing) and the new reality God will bring to pass in the future (energizing)."[8] Talk to us about proclaiming that new reality.

HW: We have a special message to proclaim in these last days of earth's history. God created our human family to live with Him eternally. We have turned away from God's ideal, but God has made a plan for us to be restored to fellowship with Him. Rather than simply inform, prophetic preaching aims to redeem and transform, to bring people back to a saving relationship with God. We don't have much time to return. That is why prophetic preaching has a sense of urgency. Here is an illustration I share with my students. If you come across a house on fire and see a mother and children trapped inside, would you stand outside and say to yourself, "Maybe I should call the fire department"? No! You would shout out with authority and spring into action no matter what the personal cost might be. The world is on fire, morally if not spiritually. It's time for prophetic preachers to step up and warn earth's inhabitants how to escape before the final conflagration and show them where to find refuge in Jesus Christ, before He comes again.

DM: What appeals to you personally about prophetic preaching?

HW: The Bible says Jesus taught "as one having authority, and not as the scribes" (Mark 1:22). Prophetic preaching appeals to me because it challenges me—in fact, it challenges all of us—to speak with authority. Jesus said to His disciples, "'All authority has been given to Me in heaven and on earth'" (Matt. 28:18), and then He gave His disciples authority to "go therefore and make disciples of all the nations" (Matt. 28:19). Many preachers seem to have lost that authority. Many preachers look more like entertainers than Spirit-filled leaders who speak with authority. A few generations ago, people looked up to preachers, viewing them as important figures of authority. Today, we are ignored and presented in the media largely as caricatures or greedy sycophants. The time has come for us to reclaim the gift of prophetic preaching. We need to step forward into the marketplace and declare, "Thus saith the Lord" so people will once again stop in their tracks and listen to what we have to say. Then they will have no option but to respond to the One who called us to declare righteousness and speak boldly against sin.

DM: Let's talk about the personal life of the prophetic preacher. An individual in Scripture who comes to mind as an example of a powerful prophetic preacher is John the Baptist. He confronted the evils of his day and called people to repent and turn to God and His ideal for their lives. He also lived with such holiness that some even wondered if he was the Messiah. How important is the personal example of the prophetic preacher in giving credibility to the message proclaimed?

HW: Not everyone called to preach prophetically will be a John the Baptist of whom Jesus Himself said, "'Truly I say to you, among those born of women there has not arisen anyone greater than John the Baptist!'" (Matt. 11:11, NASB). However, a consistent personal witness by the prophetic preacher is essential. I can also say from personal experience that God chooses some of the most unlikely, even broken, vessels to be His prophetic preachers, but they must demonstrate a personal surrender to Christ as Savior and Lord. This means that when they are tempted to compromise a little in some area, they don't; and this means that when they speak a word, there aren't members of their family sitting in the congregation saying, "Oh, you should see this person at home." They are consistently truthful to the high calling God has placed on their lives.

DM: When you look at prophetic preachers both in the Scriptures and in history, it seems there is a price to pay when you confront a culture that has departed from God's ideal.

HW: You're right. Many of those who spoke for God ended up being stoned, imprisoned, mocked, tortured, and crucified (Heb. 11). That's even true in our day. A twentieth century prophetic preacher who comes to mind is Dr. Martin Luther King Jr. Others who have paid the price are unsung heroes and heroines whose identities we will not know until Jesus comes. On one occasion, Ellen White said, as any true prophetic preacher would: "I know that which I now speak will bring me into conflict. This I do not covet, for the conflict has seemed to be continuous of late years; but I do not mean to live a coward or die a coward, leaving my work undone. I must follow in my Master's footsteps."[9] These are my sentiments also. Some people will isolate you and say, "Don't listen to that crazy preacher!" But Jesus said, "'Blessed are you when they revile you and persecute you, and say all kinds of evil against you falsely for My sake. Rejoice and be exceedingly glad, for great is your reward in heaven, for so they persecuted the prophets who were before you'" (Matt. 5:11, 12).

DM: It's certainly important to remember we're not taking this path as prophetic preachers because it's the smooth road or the popular path. What books would you recommend for pastors who want to learn more about prophetic preaching?

HW: You have already mentioned the excellent book by Leonora Tubbs Tisdale, *Prophetic Preaching: A Pastoral Approach*. That's one of the best volumes I've read on prophetic preaching. There is also a little volume by Marvin McMickle titled *Where Have All the Prophets Gone?*[10] Some other helpful books include *Voicing the Vision: Imagination and Prophetic Preaching* by Linda L. Clader[11] and *Prophetic Imagination* by Walter Brueggemann.[12]

DM: What words of encouragement would you give to a preacher who is impacted by this interview but feels afraid of what the personal cost might be?

HW: I would say, "Praise God you don't feel adequate for the task." The one who is not scared is the one who scares me. Run from the preacher who is self-confident and self-promoting. That person is a false prophet. When you sense the awesomeness of the task of prophetic preaching, you have something in common with great prophetic preachers like Jeremiah and Isaiah, who trembled in the presence of God but went forward to preach anyway, depending wholly on the power of God.

~

CHAPTER 16 — REFLECTION/DISCUSSION QUESTIONS

1. Hyveth Williams maintains that prophetic preaching critically challenges the status quo. What changes need to happen in your community?

2. How can a preacher find the courage and holy boldness to challenge long-cherished traditions and practices that are out of harmony with the Word of God?

3. What promises of Scripture provide encouragement to prophetic preachers?

Notes:

1. "Prophetic Preaching." An interview with Hyveth Williams, *Ministry* July 2011. Reprinted by permission.
2. Marvin A. McMickle, *Where Have All The Prophets Gone? Reclaiming Prophetic Preaching in America* (Cleveland, OH: The Pilgrim Press, 2006).
3. Ellen G. White, *The Southern Work* (Washington, DC: Review and Herald Pub. Assn., 1966), 9.
4. Leonora Tubbs Tisdale, *Prophetic Preaching: A Pastoral Approach* (Louisville, KY: Westminster John Knox Press, 2010), 10.
5. Ibid.
6. http://www.abyssinian.org/about-us/pastors-bio/.
7. http://www.videosurf.com/video/of-towers-and-lightsbutts-calvin-61656480.
8. Ibid.
9. White, 11.
10. (Cleveland, OH: The Pilgrim Press, 2006).
11. (Harrisburg, PA: Morehouse Publishing, 2003).
12. (Minneapolis, MN: Augsburg Fortress, 2001).

SEVENTEEN
REACHING THE SECULAR MIND

Ravi Zacharias has been called one of the great Christian thinkers of our generation. Born in India to a family whose ancestors came from the highest castes of the Hindu priesthood, Zacharias has become a powerful ambassador for Christ. His weekly radio program, "Let My People Think," is heard around the world. He has authored numerous books and articles including "Can Man Live Without God?"

DEREK MORRIS (DM): In your book, *Can Man Live Without God?*, you suggest that there has been a concerted effort by some secular thinkers to prejudice the minds of this generation against a belief in God.[1] What strategies are these secular thinkers employing to promote their antitheistic views?[2]

RAVI ZACHARIAS (RZ): Those strategies come overtly as well as subtly. The challenge to the concept of theism can be traced through certain philosophers of the last century like Nietzsche, the Huxleys, Bertrand Russell, and then the existentialist writers like Sartre and Camus.

It can also be traced with a little more subtlety though on a widespread base in certain academic settings. I could name one of the Ivy League schools which has a promotional video right now where the closing statement is given by a student saying that one of the most fulfilling results of attending that university was to become an intellectually fulfilled atheist. That is in a promotional video! You can also go to places like Oxford where people like Peter Atkins and Richard Dawkins unapologetically state that their goal is not merely to talk about the ideas of God's non-existence but to convince even those who believe that theism is essentially irrational. Dawkins, in his Voltaire Lectures to the British Humanist Association a couple years ago, talked about religious belief as being a kind of virus in the human software.

The effort to prejudice minds against a belief in God also comes through powerfully in much of the entertainment medium today. Its desacralizing of sexuality, respect for parents and family, and the sanctity of marriage, of word, of deed has a way of moving minds away from a belief in God. These sorts of notions come in rather subliminally, but people absorb them, and before you realize it, you are no longer shocked by things that ought to shock your sensitivities.

Then there are the courts and the legal system, where there is a loss of the crucial sense of life's essential value. Here both birth and death have largely lost their moral focus, and human issues are decided largely on the basis of pragmatic legal interpretations and entangled judicatory argumentation. Here the underlying ethic is often seen in terms of money or unduly influenced by the results of a survey.

The cumulative effect of all this has seemed to lower the moral convictions of young minds especially. Teenagers who have hardly gained the maturity to respond to complex moral choices are now confronted by options that fell their ethical presuppositions long before they should have the possibility of having to face them.

DM: What are some ways that secular people have sought to make sense out of life apart from God?

RZ: Nietzsche was alert to this inevitable question. He said, in his parable called "The Madman," "Is not night and more night coming on all the time? Must not lanterns be lit in the morning?"[3] In other words, the dawn of this idea was going to be a kind of darkness. What is going to lighten your path along the way? Or, as Nietzsche expressed it, "What sacred games shall we have to invent?"[4]

Malcolm Muggeridge summarized it well when he said it will be either megalomania or erotomania, the drive for power or the drive for pleasure. If God is dead or out of the picture, that is basically what we're left with. Politically, we see the drive for power, and culturally, we see the drive for pleasure. But people are too so-phisticated to simply admit that these are their most meaningful reasons for living. They dress it up. So you tend to end up with sophisticated pragmatic philosophies which direct contemporary humanity to simply do whatever works.

In reaction to the emptiness of this kind of Godless pragmatism, we see the entry of a strain of spirituality which comes in through the back door in the form of all kinds of mysticism. Some of the Eastern forms of mysticism have come in because they facilitate a form of ethics without God. So our pragmatic bent or our mystical bent become the substitute for the theistic commitment.

DM: It seems that many Christians, including preachers, are reticent to share their faith with secular people because they believe their non-Christian friends and neighbors are experiencing a fulfilling, contented existence. Yet, you suggest "for many in our high-paced world, despair is not a moment; it is a way of life."[5] Why does an antitheistic worldview so often lead to despair?

RZ: It may not be an anguished despair, but it is a surrender to a pointlessness of existence. It is Despair with a capital D. Existentialists admit that. Camus com-mented that death is philosophy's only problem. Jean-Paul Sartre said that life is an empty bubble, floating on the sea of nothingness. On his deathbed he admitted that his philosophy of atheism turned out to be unlivable. He rejected its ramifica-tions, albeit very late in life.

The reason an antitheistic worldview so often leads to despair lies deep within the human heart. Solomon said in Ecclesiastes that God has put eternity into the heart of man. We long for such a quality of coherence that denies death the capa-bility of swallowing up all the affections, all the loves we have, thus rendering life pointless. So this hunger for coherence and transcendent meaning is a very real one. The moral sense within the human mind compels us to seek a basic sense of significance, not just a contrived significance, but an essential, authentic signifi-cance. This has been observed and proven time and again.

I was invited by one of the ten wealthiest men of today to speak in Hong Kong. This man is a Chinese tycoon, a multi-billionaire. He was hosting some dinners and luncheons for what they call the diamond collar group. These are the very suc-cessful business magnates, the cream of the cream as it were. As soon as I landed at the airport, I was invited to have dinner with this gentleman, and I just threw the question across the table, "When did you become a Christian?"

He said, "Oh, about 18 months ago."

I said, "What prompted it?"

He replied, "I got out of my office building one day and was driving home. I thought to myself, 'My life is empty. I really don't have any purpose. I have all this money, but I don't have purpose in my life.'" He phoned his wife, and they decided to go to church that evening. It was a weeknight, and they walked into the midst of a discipleship training group. After attending for a few weeks, they committed their lives to Christ!

If you go to any university campus when we hold our university forums, the place is full. It is packed. We've been to Harvard, Cornell, Princeton, Ohio State, Indiana University. Wherever we go, the place is filled with students who are ready to take on challenges and ask questions. I think this is a sign of a genuine hunger. Recently, I did a Faith and Science lecture forum on God and the problem of evil. There were nearly two thousand in attendance on a weeknight. It was transmitted to nearly one hundred universities on a big screen. Over one hundred countries logged in on the Internet. This shows there is a moral sense within us that wants to put the puzzle of life together.

There are some, of course, who say "All these issues don't matter that much to me." But it seems to me that when the chips are down, they are not able to live by the logical implications of their presuppositions. They only hide from them.

DM: Well, that brings us to the radical claim of Jesus. People are looking for meaning in life, freedom from despair, and along comes Jesus and says "I am the Way, the Truth, and the Life." That claim seems strangely out of place to many in our pluralistic, postmodern society. Yet you affirm that "Jesus made a most reasonable statement when He claimed exclusivity."[6]

RZ: Truth by definition is exclusive. What people often forget, even in vast audiences, is that Christianity is not the only faith that claims exclusivity. Every religion I know claims it. Hinduism is exclusivistic in that it will not surrender the law of karma or the law of reincarnation. Buddhism was born rejecting Hinduism. Islam is obviously exclusivistic. Any time you make a truth claim, you are implying that something you have asserted conforms to reality. So truth by definition is exclusive. If a truth claim is made, the question is whether it is a valid argument or merely a whimsical assertion. When you are testing a truth claim, there needs to be logical consistency, empirical adequacy, and experiential relevance.

When Jesus made the claim to be "the Way, the Truth and the Life," He was making the claim that He, in His essential being, offered, asserted, and lived by that which conformed to ultimate reality. It is most reasonable that He made an exclusive claim. And Jesus is certainly the One who has been most tested and analyzed in history to see if His claims were true.

DM: You have asserted "the Christian message stands or falls upon the authenticity or spuriousness of the Bible."[7] So, as you are sharing with someone about the truth claim of Jesus, the witness of Scripture is crucial. What evidence would you share with a secular person that the Bible is indeed the authentic Word from God?

RZ: Here you've got 66 books, written by about 40 authors over 1,500 years! It would be very easy, if someone wanted to destroy this Book, to find a blatant array of contradictions. I find it fascinating that whenever these Scriptures are challenged in an open setting, and people talk about contradictions, at most they come up with three or four, if they come up with any of any real substance. I have yet to find anyone who has made a substantial case out of the contradictions in the Bible.

Bruce Metzger, of Princeton University, one of the leading New Testament scholars of our time, made the comment that the legitimacy of the text, based on the earliest documents and what we now have, has an astonishing 99.4 percent of accuracy. In the Bible you have placed together about 5,000 pieces or documents. Looking at the evidence you know immediately that this is not a fabricated Book, post facto.

The next thing you see is that the Bible is a historic book, not just a mystical book. For a long time, scholars would talk about the character of Pontius Pilate being without substance in extra-biblical history. All of a sudden in recent times, we have discovered mention of Pontius Pilate in extra-biblical sources.

Another evidence of the authenticity of Scripture is the claims of Christ, which are so drastic. The most dramatic claim of Jesus is the Resurrection. If there were any possibility of completely devastating the Scriptures, it seems the religious leaders and skeptics of the day could have done it on this front with a brilliant stroke of counterpoint. If the resurrection of Jesus was a myth, the disciples could have simply claimed a spiritual resurrection of Jesus, asserting that even though His body was dead, His spirit is present with us. How could you argue with that? It's a claim that has no empirical reference. But the disciples claimed a bodily resurrection, a claim that could easily have been disproved if it were not true by producing the body. The resurrection of Christ is so dramatic a claim that it made the disciples vulnerable to disproof if it were a false claim. This is not what myth is made of. Eleven out of the twelve of Jesus' followers were willing to die a martyr's death because they knew He had indeed risen from the dead, when prior to His appearance before them they had been hiding for fear.

So, in judging the validity of Scripture, you take the coherent message coming through over 1,500 years, you take the volume of documentation tracing back to the original, you take the history, the geography, the characters that are testable, and the miracles that are clearly attested to. The Scriptures are, without a doubt, a unique document.

DM: As we read the Scriptures, we discover that even the people of God are not immune to the problem of suffering. Many skeptics point to this problem of suffering as the greatest obstacle to believing in God. You address this issue in your book *Cries of the Heart* and suggest "the answer to suffering is more relational than prepositional."[8] Could you explain what you mean by that?

RZ: The problem of suffering is a most fascinating question to raise if we see ourselves to be purely the product of the random collocation of atoms. If we believe we are here by pure chance, why do we attribute a moral context to the problem of suffering? If anything, we should accept it as one of the most concrete aspects of our evolution. The reason we assign it to a moral context is that we are unable to shake off our moral nature. There is that innate moral frame of reference. To raise the problem of suffering is actually to establish the existence of a moral framework, and a moral framework doesn't exist unless a moral Lawgiver Himself does.

Beyond these considerations, I don't think the question will be answered by logic alone. I think there are propositional answers, enough to dent the question and bring about a meaningful response. When all is said and done, it is the Who of the

Bible you trust in and not just the What. It is the relationship that you lean on. There is enough in human experience to sustain that.

If you take a child into the hospital, and a big needle is about to be inserted into the arm, the child may scream and cry and grab your hand in the process, but the trust is still there. The power to keep moving on in life is born out of a relationship. Propositionally, the problem of suffering is only partially answered. The peace and the strength are found in the rational, experimental consideration of things.

DM: In your interaction with secular people, you have learned "there is no point in arguing with a person who is determined to explain everything away. Nothing good can come if the will is wrong."[9] How, then, should a Christian respond to such a person?

RZ: There are some people in whom skepticism is so embedded that even when their defenses are dropped they still have a gut level feeling that their skepticism is well founded. So you have to allow for a process, a paradigm shift. That occurs in several ways. First, by asking the person the right questions which they then are forced to live with and think through. Second, by not mocking the person's positions at that point but respecting that there is an honest seeking. Third, and I think this is very important, the church should always be an authentic worshiping community because it is in the context of authenticity and worship that barriers are most likely to fall. It has to season the relationship, not dominate it.

DM: Some years ago, you stated "communicating the Christian faith has become extremely complicated in our day. There are few accepted beliefs any more."[10] What practical counsel would you give to a person who is committed to reaching secular people with the Christian message?

RZ: Communicating the Christian faith to secular people is a genuine struggle for many in the ministry. The pastoral task today of shepherding people is, in itself, a daunting process. So the most important step, before even the apologetics and outreach begins, is to be personally and consistently replenished. If you are not replenished consistently, then your ability to minister to the person without Christ is going to be sapped.

A second step is to enable the church to be connected with society. With each enabler you produce, you are multiplying yourself exponentially. If you have a church of one hundred that is expecting you to do the outreach, it is going to be a very slow process. But if you are equipping them, you are moving on several tracks. For this reason your ministry should be challenging the church person at an intellectual and emotional level, always undergirded by the Scriptures, so they have the confidence to reach out to others.

Third, I believe those in ministry ought to be reading very widely. Expenditure of words without an income of ideas will lead to conceptual bankruptcy. So reading is not a luxury; it is a necessity. It needs to be a top priority for those of us who are dealing with ideas and people.

~

CHAPTER 17 — REFLECTION/DISCUSSION QUESTIONS

1. How deeply committed are you to reaching secular people with the saving gospel of Jesus Christ?

2. What books or journals have you read in the past year that have helped you to understand people who hold a non-Christian worldview?

3. Review your preaching over the past year. How much emphasis have you placed on connecting with secular people or equipping your hearers to connect with secular people?

Notes:

1. Ravi Zacharias, *Can Man Live With out God?* (Dallas, TX: Word Publishing, 1994), xiii.

2. "Reaching the Secular Mind." An interview with Ravi Zacharias, *Ministry* March 2000. Reprinted by permission.

3. Quoted in Ravi Zacharias, *A Shattered Visage: The Real Face of Atheism* (Grand Rapids, MI: Baker Books, 1990), 21.

4. Ibid.

5. *Can Man Live Without God?* 71.

6. Ibid., 130.

7. Ravi Zacharias, *Deliver Us From Evil: Restoring the Soul in a Disintegrating Culture* (Dallas, TX: Word Publishing, 1996), 198.

8. Ravi Zacharias, *Cries of the Heart: Bringing God Near When He Feels So Far* (Nashville, TN: Word Publishing, 1998), 89.

9. Ibid., 9.

10. *A Shattered Visage: The Real Face of Atheism,* 2.

EIGHTEEN
SEQUENCE PREACHING

H ave you ever found yourself staring at a blank sheet of paper or at a blank computer screen wondering what you'll preach next week?[1] If so, then consider sequence preaching. Preaching a series of sermons has advantages for everyone. The preacher isn't starting from ground zero every week, and the listeners have a sense of direction and purpose.

It is not difficult to convince most preachers and listeners that sequence preaching is a good idea. What may be more challenging is knowing where to begin.

A simple five-step process follows, field-tested in a local church, that will help you craft an effective sermon series.

Step #1: Select a sermon series theme

Sequence preaching can be expository or topical. One option includes picking a book from the Bible and preaching either the whole book or a portion. A second option would be to choose a topic or theme and then select a series of passages that develop your theme.

Your listeners can help you with the selection process. Many excellent ideas for expository and topical series emerge from audience analysis. You will invariably end up with more suggestions for sermon series than you can accomplish in one calendar year.[2]

Soliciting feedback from your listeners regarding a possible sermon series creates a sense of excitement and anticipation. One couple went online and purchased a book for me that they thought would be helpful for a sermon series. They were not even members of our congregation!

Step #2: Determine the number of sermons in the series

Once you have decided on a particular book or theme, determine the number of sermons that should be included. In determining the number of sermons for an expository series, thought units are more helpful guides than chapter divisions.[3] I listened to one pastor preach a series of 21 sermons on the book of John. He decided to take one chapter each week. That works reasonably well with certain books, such as Daniel, but not for the Gospel of John. Look at John 2. How many thought units can you find in that one chapter? At least two. John 2:1–11 records the miracle at Cana. John 2:12–25 records the first cleansing of the temple. Similarly, there are multiple thought units in John 3 and 4.

As a young preacher, I spent two years preaching through the Gospel of Luke. It was a welcome change from the panic of staring at a blank sheet of paper each week. My preaching passage was preselected—the next thought unit in the Gospel of Luke. The text was rich and varied, and both the preacher and the listeners enjoyed the journey through the Word of God.

Just be aware you need to choose your text carefully if you intend to preach an extended sermon series. You also need to think about the attention span of your listeners. If you spent the whole year preaching through Ecclesiastes, everyone would soon be crying out, "Vanity of vanities, all is vanity."

As a rule, I limit each series from four to six sermons.[4] We live in an era when people have short attention spans. You might need to preach on a portion of a book rather than the entire text. I have preached a six-part series on an entire book of the Bible, and I've also preached a four-part series on four verses.

An example of an expository series from Paul's letter to the Philippians follows. This series was entitled "Rejoicing in the Lord" and covered the entire epistle:

>> "Two Reasons to Rejoice," based on Phil. 1:1–11
>> "Rejoicing in the Midst of Adversity," based on Phil. 1:12–30
>> "Joy Unspeakable and Full of Glory," based on Phil. 2:1–11
>> "Rejoicing Together," based on Phil. 2:12–30

>> "Rejoicing in Jesus Alone," based on Phil. 3:1–4:1

>> "Always Rejoicing," based on Phil. 4:2–23

An example of a series on a portion of a book follows. This four-part series on James 5:13–16 was entitled "Prayer, Praise, and Healing":

>> "Is Anyone Among You Suffering?" based on James 5:13a

>> "Is Anyone Cheerful?" based on James 5:13b

>> "Is Anyone Sick?" based on James 5:14

>> "Heal Me, O Lord" based on James 5:14–16

If I had given such careful attention to the entire epistle, we could have spent several years in James. That might have been educational, but I'm sure most listeners would welcome more variety. For an expository and topical series, I preached a four-part series based on Luke 24:13–45.

The series was entitled "The Emmaus Road":

>> "The Testimony of Cleopas"

>> "The Testimony of Moses"

>> "The Testimony of the Prophets"

>> "The Testimony of the Psalmists"

Step #3: Develop a reading list

Once you decide on a series and the number of sermons in it, you are ready to develop a reading list. For both an expository and a topical series of sermons, your primary source of information should always be the inspired text. When preaching through a book or portion of Scripture, the thought unit determines the parameters of your study. For a topical series, you will look for a passage or passages of Scripture that address the subject under consideration.

As you develop your reading list, consult with at least one resource person who has expertise related to the content of the sermon series. For example, when preparing for a series of 12 messages on the Sermon on the Mount in Matthew, I consulted a New Testament scholar whose Matthew library is larger than my entire New Testament library. After we had a stimulating discussion, this New Testament scholar recommended five books that became the primary volumes on my reading list.

If you plan your preaching calendar well in advance, you can solicit the assistance of individuals far and near. With some advance planning on your part, the books on your reading list can be purchased at a great discount. I generally purchase good quality, used books online, saving time and energy.

Step #4: Create a visual motif for the sermon series

One of the advantages of sequence preaching is focusing on a particular passage or theme for an extended period. This provides the opportunity for your worship team to create a visual motif for the entire series. For example, in preparation for a six-part sermon series on Philippians, we printed several thousand parchment scrolls of the Philippian letter, which could be given to listeners. Students from the church school helped roll the scrolls, creating some anticipation and a sense of active involvement in the upcoming series. This Philippian scroll became the dominant visual motif for the series. Listeners were encouraged to actively participate during each message by reading portions of the epistle from their scroll. They were also encouraged to take their scrolls home for further study. To see worshipers coming to church each week with their copies of the Philippian scroll in their hands was a beautiful sight.

For a topical sermon series on healthy Christians, we acquired a balance beam from a local gymnastics school.[5] Members of our worship team purchased and painted large styrofoam letters that spelled out the words Healthy Christians. These letters were placed on the balance beam, along with the silhouette of a gymnast. The nonverbal message was clear: this sermon series on healthy Christians is all about balance.

Developing a powerful visual motif becomes difficult, if not impossible, if the passage or theme shifts drastically every week. Sequence preaching provides time to develop and utilize a powerful visual motif that will be remembered long after the series has ended.

Step #5: Craft a powerful preaching idea for each sermon in the series

When preaching a series, remember the basics: each message should be the communication of a single powerful idea.[6] For both expository and topical preaching, that single dominant thought should be derived from the text, and usually needs to be restated in order to make it personal, contemporary, concise, and memorable. Your preaching idea is the single dominant thought you want your listeners to remember. As your series unfolds, you might wish to take a few moments to review the preaching idea from each preceding sermon in the series.[7] This will heighten a sense of unity and progress as you lead your listeners on a journey through the Word of God.

Once you have completed the series, you have a resource members can share. At the conclusion of a ten-part expository series on the book of Daniel, we gave away more than ten thousand CDs. Doing so extends the impact of your preaching ministry. Your sermon series could also be made available on your church Web site or posted as a podcast on iTunes.[8]

Conclusion

Of course, not every church has all the resources I have mentioned here. Take what you can and apply it to your own situation. Sequence preaching has been practiced for centuries, and for good reason. The next time you find yourself staring at a blank sheet of paper or a blank computer screen, consider implementing this simple five-step process for the design and preparation of an effective sermon series.

~

CHAPTER 18 — REFLECTION/DISCUSSION QUESTIONS

1. What is the most significant sermon series you have heard or preached?

2. How can sequence preaching enhance your preaching ministry?

3. What new insights have you learned from this chapter that will help you with your next sermon series?

Notes:

1. "Sequence Preaching: How to design and prepare an effective sermon series." *Ministry*, December 2008. Reprinted by permission.

2. For more information about a sermon planning group, see Chapter 25.

3. There are rare occasions when chapter divisions and thought units run parallel to each other. When preparing a series of messages on the book of Daniel, I discovered that the first nine chapters of the book of Daniel are distinct thought units. Daniel 10–12, on the other hand, is a single thought unit. With this in mind, I developed a ten-part sermon series on the book of Daniel. This series can be viewed online at www.forest-lakechurch.org. Manuscripts of this ten-part expository sermon series are available at www.powerfulbiblicalpreaching.com.

4. My longest sermon series in recent years was a 13-part series on the Ten Commandments, entitled, "Words of Blessing: A Fresh Look at the Ten Commandments." When planning the series, I sensed that I would need at least ten sermons, one for each commandment. I chose to add a first-person narrative at the beginning of the series to set some historical background and to conclude the series with two additional sermons: one on "The Two Great Commandments" according to the teachings of Jesus, and a final sermon called "Disposable?" which addressed the issue of the perpetuity of the moral law. I was pleasantly surprised to see that the listeners maintained interest and focus for the entire 13-part series.

5. The Healthy Christians series was comprised of six messages: "Healthy Lifestyles," "Healthy Families," "Healthy Finances," "Healthy Relationships," "Healthy Bodies," and "Healthy Minds." The Healthy Christians sermon manuscripts are available at www.powerfulbiblicalpreaching.com.

6. Jesus modeled the importance of communicating a single dominant idea. See Chapter 1 and Chapter 8.

7. Manuscripts of this four-part expository sermon series are available at www.powerfulbiblicalpreaching.com.

8. For more information about extending the impact of your preaching ministry, see "Preaching to the World" in the July 2007 issue of *Ministry*. Available at www.ministrymagazine.org.

NINETEEN
FIRST-PERSON NARRATIVE PREACHING

Many of your elderly church members have heard more sermons than you will ever preach.[1] When someone speaks of Daniel in the lions' den, or David and Goliath, they already know "the rest of the story." How can we retell these powerful biblical narratives in a way that will impact all our listeners, including those who have heard them over and over?

Let me suggest a fresh approach: first-person narrative preaching.[2]

Another angle

When preparing a first-person narrative sermon, you must ask yourself this question: "Where shall I stand in the story?" If you are retelling the story of Paul's missionary visit to Philippi, will you be the apostle Paul, Lydia (an influential member of the church in Philippi), or the Philippian jailer? The character you choose will obviously affect your perspective as you retell the story.

In a six-part series on Paul's epistle to the Philippians, I opted to use a first-person narrative sermon to begin the series. My goal was to introduce the letter and provide some helpful historical and cultural background regarding the city of Philippi and Paul's ministry there.

With this goal in mind, I chose a place to stand in the story. I would be Epaphroditus, an elder of the church in Philippi. Listen now, as I share the old, old story from a fresh perspective.

Epaphroditus's story

Grace and peace to you, my brother.[3] Grace and peace to you, my sister. Grace and peace to all of you from God our Father and the Lord Jesus Christ. I did not expect to meet you on the Via Appia. I am Epaphroditus, from Macedonia. I make my home in the city of Philippi. In fact, I am on my journey home right now.

You may wonder why I'm dressed like a Roman if I come from Macedonia. Well, I've been in Rome for some time, visiting our spiritual father, the apostle Paul. The Christian brothers and sisters in Philippi sent me to Rome when they heard the apostle Paul had been put under house arrest. They knew he would need provisions and someone to care for him. I've been in Rome for some time now. That's one reason why I'm dressed like a Roman.

But I am also dressed like a Roman because I'm a citizen of Rome. You see, Philippi is a Roman colony. Let me tell you a little about my city. Strategically positioned on the great east-west trade route across Macedonia, Philippi was founded almost seven hundred years ago. It was originally called "Small Fountains" because of the springs of water that flow out of the base of the hill on which the city was built. Philippi was fortified by King Philip of Macedonia almost four hundred years ago. That's where our city gets its new name: Philippi. Modest King Philip named the city after himself!

For the past two hundred years, Philippi has been a Roman colony and known more as a military outpost than a trading center. There are two parts to the city. The upper part, on the side of a hill, overlooks the fertile valley of the Gangites River. The theater and the acropolis are located on the upper part of the city. In the lower part of the city, you'll find the forum and the marketplace. And right between the upper and lower city runs the Via Egnatia, the east-west trade route. Philippi is only about a two-hour walk from the coast. You just take the Via Egnatia east to Neapolis. Well, as you can see, I'm very proud of my city.

As you can tell from my name, Epaphroditus, I was not born into a family that worshiped the God of heaven, the Father of our Lord and Savior Jesus Christ. Some people have told me my name means "lovely" or "handsome," but I've discovered it's actually in honor of the Greek goddess of love, Aphrodite. Epi means "on" or "before." So Epaphroditus means "one who is before the goddess of love." Devoted to Aphrodite. I've often wished I had been born into a family that worshiped the God of heaven and been given a name like Timotheos, "honored by

God," or Theophilus, "loved by God." I even thought about giving myself a new name, but even if I don't have a new name, I do have a new heart. I have become a follower of the Lord Jesus Christ, and if anyone is in Christ, he is a new creation. That's what the apostle Paul said in his letter to the believers in Corinth. A new creation. And I am rejoicing in the Lord!

I first heard the good news about Jesus Christ when the apostle Paul came to my city, Philippi. That was more than ten years ago now. Perhaps twelve or thirteen years. Time passes so quickly! It was quite an eventful visit. A few days after Paul and his companion Silas arrived in Philippi, they went down to the Gangites River, just south of the city. There they met several women who were gathered for prayer, including a devout woman named Lydia. She is quite an influential person in Philippi and trades in purple cloth from the city of Thyatira. Lydia and her family received the message about Jesus Christ with an open heart, and they were baptized in the name of the Lord Jesus Christ, right there in the river! She even invited Paul and Silas to stay at her home.

As they continued their ministry in Philippi, Paul and Silas met a slave girl. I don't remember her name. She was controlled by an evil spirit, but she made a great deal of money for her owners by fortune-telling. This slave girl kept following Paul and Silas wherever they went, shouting, "These men are servants of the Most High God, who are telling you the way to be saved." That sounded good at first. After all, it was true. But the slave girl just kept shouting over and over again. People couldn't hear what Paul was saying about Jesus. Finally, Paul got very upset. Not with the slave girl, you understand, but with the evil spirit. Paul rebuked the spirit that was controlling her and commanded it to leave in the name of Jesus Christ.

That's when the trouble started. The "owners" of the slave girl had been making a lot of money through her fortune-telling, and they were angry that their business had ended so abruptly. They didn't care about the slave girl. Just about themselves. So they stirred up the crowd and had Paul and Silas arrested, publicly beaten, and thrown in jail.

What happened next was truly amazing. Paul and Silas were thrown in the inner dungeon and their feet were fastened in the stocks. It was dark. Damp. It smelled like a sewer. All around them were the sounds of cursing prisoners. But instead of complaining, Paul and Silas started singing, because even though it was dark in the prison, the light of Jesus was in their hearts. Hallelujah! That's a Hebrew word, you know. I don't know much Hebrew, but I like that word! Hallelujah! It means "Praise the Lord!"

And that's exactly what Paul and Silas were doing. They were praising the Lord. Then at midnight, the God of heaven worked a mighty miracle. He shook the foundations of the prison with a great earthquake. But it was no ordinary earthquake. The prison didn't collapse and kill them all. No. This was a special kind of earthquake. All the doors of the prison popped open and all the prisoners' chains fell off.

That earthquake not only shook up the prison; it shook up the jailer too. He was so distressed, he was about to fall on his sword. After all, if you lose a prisoner, you pay with your own life. Then he heard a voice cry out in the darkness. "Don't harm yourself! We're all here!" Well, the jailer knew that something supernatural was going on. There were no lights. How could anyone see what he was about to do? The jailer called for a light, ran in to the inner dungeon and fell down trembling before Paul and Silas. He cried out, "Sirs, what must I do to be saved?"

Paul told the jailer about Jesus Christ. He told him that everyone who calls upon the name of the Lord will be saved. He told him that if you confess with your mouth that Jesus is Lord and believe in your heart that God has raised Him from the dead you will be saved. He told him that, just as the prophet Isaiah had predicted, Jesus was wounded for our iniquities. He was bruised for our transgressions. The punishment that brought us peace was upon Him, and with His stripes we are healed. All we like sheep have gone astray and the Lord has laid upon Him the iniquity of us all.

Well, the jailer and his family received the good news about Jesus with gladness, and they also became followers of the Lord Jesus Christ and were baptized that very night.

The apostle Paul came to visit us again several years later and encouraged us in the faith. We could tell he loved us as his own children, and we loved him too. So when our church family in Philippi heard Paul had been taken to Rome to stand trial and was under house arrest, they decided to send me to Rome to bring provisions and offer support.

But instead of being a help, I became a problem. I'm not as young as I used to be, and I think the long journey was too much for me. I became very sick. In fact, I almost died. When my church family back in Philippi heard about my sickness, they were very concerned about me. This may sound strange to some people, especially unbelievers, but I actually feel closer to my church family than to my own family. My church family loves me and cares for me as my father and mother, brothers and sisters!

And, as I said, they were very concerned about me. So Paul decided I should return to my home city of Philippi. He wanted to send a letter to the church family, and he knew they would be happy to see me and to know that I have recovered from my sickness. So he asked me to deliver his letter to them. And here it is. Now one very important rule a courier must follow is this: You must never read the contents of the document you are carrying. But the apostle Paul gave me permission to read this letter because he said it is also addressed to me. So I get to read it before everyone else.

The letter starts out like this. Why don't you follow along? I understand someone made a copy for you too.[4] Why don't we read it together? Let's start reading at the beginning of the scroll. "Paul and Timothy, servants of Christ Jesus, to all the saints in Christ Jesus at Philippi...."[5]

Reliving the story

This example of a first-person narrative illustrates that you don't simply retell the story in first-person narrative preaching. You relive the story! The preacher relives the story as one of the characters. The listeners relive the story as active participants. First-person narrative preaching can be a life-changing experience for both the preacher and the listeners.

I remember when I was preaching a first-person narrative sermon about Noah. As I relived that part of my story when the door of the ark was closing, I began to weep. The door of the ark was closing, and most of the people were still outside. In that moment, I experienced Noah's anguish of heart. As I looked up, I noticed that members of the congregation were weeping. They too were reliving the story.

I always wondered if the senior members of the congregation would be resistant to this new sermon form. After all, this is a major departure from a more traditional approach. I was surprised to discover that the senior members of the congregation, along with the children, appreciated first-person narrative preaching. They had heard the biblical stories over and over again. First-person narrative preaching gave them an opportunity to relive the biblical narrative in a fresh, life-changing way.

The preparation process for a first person narrative sermon will require at least as much time as a more traditional sermon. And, you must do a careful exegesis of your biblical texts. If you are citing portions of Scripture, you need to memorize them.

Occasionally, as in the case of Epaphroditus, you will be able to read the words of Scripture from a scroll. While you don't have to dress in authentic costume, this will make it easier for both the preacher and the listeners to relive the story.

Try a first-person narrative sermon as part of a sermon series on a book of the Bible. You won't want to use this sermon form every week, but when you are covering a familiar narrative, a first-person narrative sermon can help both the preacher and the listeners relive the story.

~

CHAPTER 19 — REFLECTION/DISCUSSION QUESTIONS

1. Consider the story of the wedding miracle at Cana. Many of your hearers are well acquainted with this narrative (John 2:1-11). How might you relive this story as a first-person narrative sermon in order to provide a fresh perspective for your hearers?

2. What is your favorite Bible story? How might you share that story as a first-person narrative?

3. Share a time when you listened to or preached a first-person narrative sermon. What lessons did you learn from that experience?

Notes:

1. "First-Person Narrative Preaching." *Ministry* May 2008. Reprinted by permission.

2. With first-person narrative preaching, it is necessary to preach without notes. For a helpful five-step process that will prepare you to preach without notes, see Chapter 23.

3. I began this first-person narrative by entering from the rear of the sanctuary and walking down the center aisle of the church. I stopped on my journey to greet my listeners.

4. Each listener received a copy of the Philippian letter when entering the sanctuary. This enabled the listeners to read with me. I was also able to challenge them to read the entire letter in the coming week.

5. Phil.1:1, (NIV). A complete written copy of this sermon is available at www.powerfulbiblicalpreaching.com. The sermon is titled "Two Reasons to Rejoice" and is part one of the Philippian series, Rejoicing in the Lord.

TWENTY
THE ART OF DOUBLE LISTENING

For more than 50 years, John R. W. Stott was Rector and Rector Emeritus of All Souls Church in London, England. He authored numerous books including his best-selling text Between Two Worlds: The Art of Preaching in the Twentieth Century. He was recognized as one of the top twelve "most effective preachers in the English-speaking world."

DEREK MORRIS (DM): Dr. Stott, I really appreciate your willingness to share with us your thinking about relevant biblical preaching.[1] In your book on preaching, entitled *Between Two Worlds,* there is one sentence that particularly caught my attention: "Humble listening is indispensable to relevant preaching."[2] Could we begin there?

JOHN R. W. STOTT (JS): I'm glad you picked that out. Actually I would like to talk now about double listening.[3] By double listening, I mean listening, of course, to God and to the Word of God, but listening to the voices of the modern world as well. Now, I make it clear that in listening to the modern world, we are not listening with the same degree of respect as that with which we listen to the voice of God. We listen to Him in order to believe and obey what He says. We listen to the modern world, not in order to believe and obey what it says, but in order to understand its cries of pain, the sighs of the oppressed. Relevant communication grows out of this process of double listening.

DM: Does this double listening begin by first listening to God?

JS: I don't know that it must be first. I think if we listen to the voices of the modern world, we grow in an understanding and appreciation of their pain and their misunderstanding of the gospel. The more aware we are of the context around us, the more urgent becomes our listening to God in order to hear a word from Him relevant to their pain. So I don't know that it matters which comes first or whether you're listening to both simultaneously. The important thing is to listen to both and not only to one. Of course, the liberal tends to listen only to modernity, and the conservative tends to listen only to God. It is the double listening that seems to me to be most needed.

DM: Let's talk about some ways you have sought to listen carefully to the modern world. One of the exciting concepts you mention in your book *Between Two Worlds* is the idea of a reading group. Could you share with us about the focus of a reading group?

JS: Well, in this business of relevance, I felt that I myself, and probably my friends, spent enough time studying the Word and theological books that helped us to understand the Word. My major weakness was a lack of understanding of the modern mind, of what was actually going on around me. So the purpose of starting the reading group was very deliberately to oblige us to listen more attentively and intelligibly to the modern world. I invited about 15 young professional people in our congregation to join the reading group: a couple doctors, a couple lawyers, an architect, and a BBC person, etc., all of whom were committed to the biblical gospel, and all of whom were modern young men and women eager to relate the gospel to the modern world. We used to meet every other month, and we still meet over 20 years later.[4] We met only last week, when, for example, we studied a book on economics: *The State We're In,* by Will Mutton.[5] The book before that was *The Selfish Gene,* by Richard Dawkins.[6]

DM: What determines the books you read?

JS: It is spontaneous from the group, and we try to be up-to-date. We studied a number of New Age books. These are not Christian books about the New Age, but actual New Age books. We read them in order to understand what New Age is really saying and thinking. I normally let others in the reading group choose, because they are much more closely in touch with these books than I am. At the end of each evening we debate what will be next.

DM: So what is the focus of your discussion? Let's say you read this book on economics. What do you hope to get out of the reading besides an awareness of what the book says? Is there discussion regarding how to respond to it in a Christian way?

JS: Yes, we begin by going around the room. Everybody is given maybe 30 seconds to identify the major issue they felt the book raises for Christian people. Then at the end of the evening we ask ourselves the question "What has the gospel to say to people who think like this?" The reading group doesn't always answer this question as sharply as I think they should, but that is the purpose, the aim of doing it.

DM: If someone were to try to get a reading group started, what suggestions would you make about the formation of a group?

JS: When I lecture on preaching, I often mention the reading group concept. I suggest that if you haven't got enough professional people in your congregation, then share with two or three other congregations, including two or three ministers. I think it could be done almost anywhere.

DM: In addition to your reading group, I noticed you also utilized ad hoc sermon resource groups from your series of sermons on issues facing Christians. This is another example of seeking to listen carefully to the modern world. Could you share with us why you formed these resource groups?

JS: Yes, it was the sense that in relating the Word to the world, I probably knew the Word more thoroughly and deeply than the congregation did because it was obviously my study. But I felt that the areas in which I was relating the Word to the world were in many cases areas about which I was ignorant. I recognized there were professional members in the congregation who were much more knowledgeable than I, and to have an ad hoc group of experts in their field would be very valuable.[7] So usually my study assistant would gather the group together. He would gather about eight people, and very often on a Sunday afternoon we would have two to two and a half hours together. I would ask them questions because I knew, roughly speaking, how I was going to handle the topic. Then I would sit back and listen to them as they debated the answer. For example, one resource group dealt with the issue of work and unemployment.

DM: Yes, and if I remember your book correctly, you had an employer, a personnel controller, and the chaplain to the Oxford Street stores as part of your resource group.

JS: And two people who experienced periods of unemployment and knew the trauma.[8]

DM: At this point you were not asking them how to interpret Scripture; you were asking them to discuss an issue about which they were well informed.

JS: Yes, and there was a different resource group for each topic. Obviously, one couldn't do that weekly, but one could do it monthly or quarterly.[9]

DM: A third way you have sought to listen to the modern world is by soliciting feedback regarding your sermons. Where did you get the idea of asking certain people in your congregation to be "lay critics"?

JS: At seminary or theological college, as we call it in Britain, there is a sermon class or homiletics group in which maybe a dozen of one's peers come and listen to one's preaching. Then on the following day they tear your sermon to pieces. So the idea of having critics is not new, but the idea of continuing the process after one graduates is fairly unusual. Most students are very glad when that time is over!

DM: But you chose medical students to serve as lay critics for evaluation and feedback regarding your sermons.

JS: Yes. I suppose a married man's wife or a married woman's husband might be an excellent lay critic. But if, like me, you're a bachelor, then you badly need critics to listen. I deliberately chose two medical students. They are trained in unbiased observation, and I thought they would be in a position to be objective and detached in their evaluation. And of course, I made sure they believed the gospel.

DM: What kind of feedback did you receive from them?

JS: Well, obviously the practical things were there, about one's gestures, or one's voice, or one's demeanor in the pulpit—all that obvious stuff. But in addition, they were highly intelligent and evangelically well-educated young men, so I was quite happy for them to comment on how I handled the text, whether they thought my hermeneutical principles were sound, and whether they agreed with the interpretation of the text.

DM: So you gave them freedom to respond in any way?

JS: Absolutely, to anything, and I asked them to put it in writing. The process was helpful.

DM: One fourth way you have sought to listen carefully was in developing your preaching syllabus, or preaching calendar. How does that work?

JS: The staff goes away two or three times a year for a whole day. One of the topics on the agenda for that day is our preaching for the next six months, or whatever the time period is. Very often we invite two or three leading laypeople to join us. We ask ourselves the question "Where are we as a congregation in terms of spiritual development and pilgrimage, and what is it that we need?" Out of that debate comes a decision as to what we are going to do next. Normally it would be a choice of a book to expound, and one of the staff may go away and divide the book into sections, suggest titles, and how it is to be handled. Sometimes that process will be done in the group. The laypeople are very important, then, because they get feedback from the wider laity. A box is also placed at the back of the church asking people to suggest sermons, topics, or books. Guidance also comes through our own pastoral counseling with people, where we come to realize their misunderstandings or a need for further enlightenment in some areas.

DM: This process of developing the preaching calendar seems to be sending an important message to the congregation: you want to listen to them.[10] It could also indicate to the congregation that the church has a specific direction it is seeking to take.

JS: Yes, that's right, and that we are taking the trouble to prepare and think about things, not operating in a haphazard way.

DM: What would you say to pastors who feel so overwhelmed in ministry they believe they don't have the time for double listening or for the preparation of relevant biblical sermons?

JS: Well, I would say that every generation needs to relearn the lesson of Acts 6. While we are not apostles, some of the pastoral duties of the apostolate do devolve upon us, particularly in the handling of the Word of God. It's absolutely essential we should concentrate on that and not allow ourselves to be distracted by administration. Preach on Acts 6 so the congregation can understand it's their responsibility to set the pastor free to preach the Word!

~

CHAPTER 20 — REFLECTION/DISCUSSION QUESTIONS

1. How would you respond to Stott's assertion that "humble listening is indispensable to relevant preaching?"

2. What is your greatest challenge in relating God's unchanging Word to our ever-changing world?

3. What suggestions in this interview did you find most helpful?

Notes:

1. "Relevant Biblical Preaching: the art of double listening." An interview with John R. W. Stott, *Ministry* January 1997. Reprinted by permission.

2. John R. W. Stott, *Between Two Worlds: The Art of Preaching in the Twentieth Century* (Grand Rapids, MI: William B. Eerdmans, 1982), p. 192.

3. Dr. Stott amplified this idea in a more recent publication, *The Contemporary Christian: An Urgent Plea for Double Listening* (Leicester, England: Inter-Varsity Press, 1992); the American printing is also by IVP, 1992, and is entitled simply The Contemporary Christian.

4. The reading group meeting schedule changed to four times per year.

5. Will Hutton, *The State We're In* (London, England: Vintage, 1996).

6. Richard Dawkins, *The Selfish Gene* (New York, NY: Oxford University Press, 1989). Dawkins is an Oxford professor who espouses atheistic and Darwinian views.

7. Dr. Stott suggested that if sufficient or appropriate resource people are not available in a particular congregation, people in the community can be utilized.

8. One of these unemployed individuals had applied for 43 jobs, had been granted only six interviews, and was still without work.

9. For a more detailed consideration of a sermon resource group, see Chapter 21.

10. For a more detailed consideration of a sermon planning process, see Chapter 25.

TWENTY-ONE
UNLEASHING YOUR CONGREGATION'S CREATIVITY

Have you ever wondered about the effectiveness of your weekly sermon?[1] Would you like some help? Try unleashing the creative energies of your congregation.

Utilize sermon resource groups

I first learned of this strategy from John R.W. Stott.In his book *Between Two Worlds*, Stott describes the pre-sermon dialogue as follows: "The discussion was invariably lively, and on a number of occasions I found myself sitting back and listening to the debate as it developed between different opinions. Eavesdropping in this way proved extremely stimulating and enlightening."[2] "I would tend to ask them questions because I knew, roughly speaking, how I was going to handle the topic. And I would then sit back and listen to them as they debated the answer."[3]

The diverse composition of these sermon resource groups added richness to Stott's preaching, as he prepared his series, Issues Facing Britain. When thrashing out the topic of work and unemployment, Stott noted that the members of the sermon resource group "helped me to feel what they felt—the shock, the rejection, the hurt, the humiliation, and the sense of helplessness, which are all caused by unemployment."[4] He noted that "the whole experience was creative, as we struggled to relate biblical principles and contemporary contexts to one another."[5]

I recently experimented with this strategy for preparing relevant biblical sermons on Christianity in the Marketplace.[6] The series consisted of four sermons: "Being

Christian in the Classroom," "Being Christian in the Care-Giving Professions," "Being Christian in Business," and "Being Christian at Home." In preparation for each of these sermons, I met with a sermon resource group on the Tuesday evening prior to the preaching of the sermon.

Being Christian in the classroom

There were five individuals in the first sermon resource group, discussing being Christian in the classroom: a university ethics professor, a public high school English teacher, an elementary school teacher, a university sophomore, and an academy sophomore.

We met for 75 minutes, and the results were amazing. I learned from Stott my primary purpose in that session was to listen. It was immediately apparent that many members of the resource group had experienced times when teachers were not Christian in the classroom.

Nadine, the elementary school teacher, shared a troubling story about a traumatic event she experienced in eighth grade. Her teacher would slam a wooden yardstick on his desk, just to watch the students jump. On one occasion, he marched into the classroom with a roll of tape with which he wrapped an unsuspecting student's hands and book to the student's desk. Next, he proceeded to wrap tape around the student's head. Then the teacher stood back and laughed.

As Nadine related this experience to the resource group, I noticed the expressions of shock on their faces. This was a dramatic example of not being Christian in the classroom.

I used this story in the sermon that week, asking Nadine to share it personally. The congregation was obviously engrossed as I walked over to Nadine with a roving microphone, and gave her the opportunity to share her experience.

Another powerful illustration came from the high school English teacher. Monte told the group of a letter from a student whose life was impacted by his teaching. This story was a powerful, positive example of being Christian in the classroom. Other resource group members asked him to bring the letter to church. Monte told his experience at the close of the sermon. The congregation was palpably moved as Monte read the letter from a public high school student whose life had been transformed by a teacher who was Christian in the classroom.

Sixty-one teachers came forward at the end of the sermon for a prayer of blessing.

They responded to the challenge to be Christian in the classroom, to teach with passion and to treat their students with compassion. Before the church service was over, people were volunteering to serve on remaining sermon resource groups for the series.

A teacher, whose life had been profoundly impacted by the sermon, sent me an email, suggesting her husband's name for the sermon on "Being Christian in Business." I realized that this strategy was unleashing the creative energies of the congregation.

Being Christian in the care-giving professions

The second sermon resource group met the following Tuesday evening. The discussion focused on the theme of "Being Christian in the Care-Giving Professions." I could sense the energy in the group. The group consisted of a physician, three nurses, a school counselor, and the coordinator of spiritual care for nurses at a Christian hospital.

Again, my primary self assignment was to listen. Time passed quickly as I heard stories of care-givers driving home in tears, overwhelmed by the tidal wave of human need that seemed to engulf them.

Someone in the group referred to Mark 6 where Jesus and His disciples were moved by the needs of people. In that story we found both a vivid description of the problem and a divinely inspired solution: Christian care-givers must allow Jesus to care for them if they are to have anything to offer a needy world.

Next, they must open themselves to Christ, allowing Him to direct them regarding the when and how of caring for others. Then they can follow the way of Jesus and care unconditionally. The Christian care-givers in the congregation were challenged to care for others as Jesus cares for them.

Being Christian in business

By the third week, teachers and care-givers who had been out of town were asking for copies of "their" sermon. Something wonderful was taking place.

The third sermon resource group addressed the challenge of "Being Christian in Business." This group consisted of a businessman who operated a small family-owned auto transmission shop, an entrepreneur with graduate training in business who operated four businesses, a computer consultant who had experience in several business settings, a dentist's wife who assisted in the management of her husband's practice, and the owner/manager of a travel agency.

The group spent a lot of time discussing the challenges of being Christian in business. At the end of the 75-minute session, I felt rather bewildered. This experience reminded me that the sermon resource group members don't write the sermon for you. The group serves only as a catalyst, raising the challenges and opportunities of the marketplace in which they live and work.

After a time of prayerful reflection on my session with this sermon resource group, I was led to the narrative in Luke 19, which records the encounter of Jesus with a self-serving secular capitalist named Zacchaeus. I discovered two significant changes that occurred in his life as a result of the encounter with Jesus.

Zacchaeus experienced a change of attitude and a change of ethics. His attitude changed toward his business. No longer was he obsessed with money, but rather with the opportunity to serve. Instead of taking advantage of his clients, he sought to treat them as he would like to be treated.

At the end of the service, it was a beautiful sight to watch a variety of business people respond to the invitation to honor Jesus Christ in their businesses.

Being Christian at home

The final sermon in the series on Christianity in the Marketplace dealt with "Being Christian at Home."

Seven individuals joined me on Tuesday evening to make up this sermon resource group. Their ages ranged from a young mother in her early thirties to a grandmother in her late sixties. As I listened to the group interact, it became apparent that being Christian at home was the greatest challenge of all.

Several group members shared painful stories of hypocrisy at home, where private behavior contradicted public profession. There were tears in one group member's eyes as she shared the story of being abused by her father, a professed Christian and church member. As I looked around, I noticed tears in the eyes of other members of the group. We realized that this was a story that needed to be told as part of the sermon.

As you may know, the word "hypocrite" comes from a word describing the ancient Greek plays. The actor who concealed his true identity behind a mask was called a hupocrite. One of the members of the sermon resource group purchased a masquerade mask, and at various times during the sermon when I spoke about hypocrisy, I covered my face with the mask.

I shared three steps for avoiding hypocrisy and manifesting a Christian spirit at home: Admit you are a sinner in constant need of God's grace; extend forgiveness to others just as God has forgiven you; and recognize together the need to grow in grace.

The sermon concluded with a testimony by another member of the sermon resource group. Nancy shared her experience of becoming friends with a couple who were a wonderful example of being Christian at home.

When this couple had children, Nancy worked as their baby sitter. At one point, Nancy said to a family member, "If Len had a younger brother, I'd marry him!" Well, Nancy is now married to Len's younger brother Larry! The congregation laughed as Nancy shared the end of her story. The lesson was clear. While hypocrisy causes serious damage at home, being Christian at home results in great blessings.

Experiment with sermon resource groups

I found this experiment with sermon resource groups an exhilarating experience. The groups could be utilized in a variety of ways.

Both my series, Christianity in the Marketplace, and Stott's Issues Facing Britain, were topical in nature. A sermon resource group would also be helpful when preaching an expository series. In this setting, the composition of the group might not change each week, but rather group members might serve for the duration of a series.

Resource group members could be given the preaching passage to study for the upcoming sermon. In the group meeting, they could then discuss questions that arise from their study. What does the text mean? How does it apply to my life today? Personal experiences and stories might emerge that shed light on the biblical concept under discussion.

The use of a sermon resource group as a strategy for the preparation of relevant biblical sermons is not limited to large congregations. Stott says: "I am very reluctant to concede that even the small inner-city church and its hard-pressed pastor can manage nothing. If a carefully considered sermon on a current issue is impossible quarterly, is it really impossible annually? And if a congregation cannot produce from its own membership mature Christians who are specialists in their field, there must surely be some within reach who belong to other churches, but who would be willing to contribute their expertise to an occasional discussion group, and would even be surprised and gratified to be asked to do so."[7]

A sermon resource group is by no means a crutch for lazy or careless preachers. The group will not write the sermon for the pastor. This process does not do away with the need for careful exegesis. However, I am convinced the use of a sermon resource group will unleash the creative energies of your congregation.

According to Stott, "It is not just that the laity ask the questions and we answer them, since we too have to ask our questions for them to answer. It is rather that, by asking each other questions, we from the biblical perspective and they from the contemporary, we may together discern what answers should be given if the Word is to be contextualized in the world."[8]

~

CHAPTER 21 — REFLECTION/DISCUSSION QUESTIONS

1. Describe your most creative sermon or sermon series. Who assisted you in the preparation process?

2. List 5 of the most creative people in your congregation. How could those individuals help you with the preparation of powerful biblical sermons?

3. What insights from this chapter will impact your sermon planning and preparation?

Notes:

1. "Start a Sermon Resource Group: Unleashing your congregations Creativity." *Ministry* September 2003. Reprinted by permission.

2. John R.W. Stott, *Between Two Worlds: The Art of Preaching in the Twentieth Century* (Grand Rapids, MI: William B. Eerdmans, 1982), 199.

3. Interview with John R.W. Stott, August 12, 1996, by Derek J. Morris. Cited in Listening to the Listener: Audience Feedback as a Resource for Relevant Biblical Preaching. D.Min. thesis, Gordon-Conwell Theological Seminary, 1998, 111.

4. Stott, 199.

5. Ibid.

6. Sermon manuscripts are available at www.powerfulbiblcalpreaching.com.

7. Stott, 200.

8. Ibid., 200-201.

TWENTY-TWO
LEARNING FROM THE MARKETPLACE

Patricia Fripp is an executive speech coach, award-winning professional speaker, and former president of the National Speakers Association.

DEREK MORRIS (DM): As an award-winning professional speaker and executive speech coach, you have learned many practical pointers in the marketplace that can help preachers connect more effectively with their audiences and congregations. Let's start by considering the opening sentences of the sermon. You encourage your clients to "start with a bang" and "come out punching." Why is a strong introduction so important?

PATRICIA FRIPP (PF): Today's audiences have very short attention spans. The first and last thirty seconds have the most impact. Don't waste those precious seconds with trivialities. Come out punching.

In my speakers' schools, I teach 32 ways to open a speech. These would also be true for a sermon. You might start with a story, an interesting statistic, a startling statement—anything rather than something predictable. Being too predictable can be boring.

With the advent of the TV remote control, no one watches anything that stands still long enough to bore. Today's audiences will forgive you for anything except being boring.

We must keep our audience's needs in mind. In the first sentence or so, you want people in your audience to elbow their neighbors and say, "This is going to be good. I'm glad we're here!" When a sermon is immediately compelling, it's as if you forget everything else. It's important to memorize the first three or four sentences of your introduction. This allows you to start fluently, connecting with your audience.

DM: A common question clients ask you is how to relax before a talk. What are some practical ways a preacher can relax before the sermon and start "warmed up" rather than taking precious moments at the beginning of the sermon to get up to speed?

PF: It's totally natural to be nervous, but there are some physical exercises that can help you channel your nervousness into energy before you speak. Comedian Robin Williams does jumping jacks! I would suggest you at least physically shake the tension out of your body. Find someplace private and wave your hands in the air. Shake your hands to shake out the tension. This will help your hand movements to be much more relaxed and appropriate.

Shake your feet. Stand on one leg and shake the other. When you put your foot back on the ground, it's going to feel lighter than the other one. Now, switch legs and shake the other foot. Relax your jaw and shake your head from side to side. I shake my face so my lips and face are relaxed. Warm up your face muscles by chewing in a highly exaggerated way.

Facial relaxation is particularly important if you're speaking at a place where image magnification is being used. These simple exercises will help a preacher channel nervousness into energy.

A wonderful preparation technique for small meetings is to go around shaking hands and making eye contact with everybody beforehand. For larger meetings, shake hands with people in the front row and some of the people as they come in the door. Connect with people personally prior to your sermon. Once you've met the audience, or at least some of them, they become less scary.

DM: You emphasize the importance of connecting emotionally as well as intellectually with your audience. What are some ways a speaker can do that?

PF: In three ways. The first is *eye contact*. I suggest that a preacher begin the sermon by focusing on one person for the opening sentence. During the sermon, make sure your eye contact is at least three seconds per person, and often longer, depending on the size of your congregation.

If you are speaking to a large congregation, then look in certain directions for 3-5 seconds, and people will think you are looking at them. When you have extended eye contact with one part of the congregation and then look to another part of the congregation, people will follow you. If you have notes, complete your thought, then look down at the next note. Allow that pause to be a time for reflection for the congregation.

A second way to emotionally connect with your audience is by *telling stories*. As screenwriter Robert McKee says, "Stories are the creative conversion of life itself into a more powerful, clearer, more meaningful experience." Stories need to be populated with flesh-and-blood characters the congregation can relate to, and they need to be told well. An audience will always prefer a trivial story well told, to a brilliant story badly told. Relate your stories to the needs and interests of your congregation.

A third way to emotionally connect is what I call the *I-You ratio*. Involve your congregation in your sermon. Instead of saying, "When I was growing up, my father gave me this advice," you might say, "I don't know what advice your father gave you when you were growing up, but mine always said..." In that way, you have involved your audience. When they walk away, they have the advice your father gave you and the advice their father gave them. You might say, "Imagine how Jesus felt when..." or "Let's go back together to the fateful night when..." You're taking your congregation along with you.

DM: Let's go back for a moment to the matter of telling stories. You challenge speakers to develop their storytelling abilities. What are the ingredients of a good story, and how should a person relate that story for maximum impact?

PF: The ingredients of a good story are interesting characters, sparkling dialogue, and a dramatic lesson learned. The dramatic lesson learned is the point of the story. The funniest or most exhilarating story will be pointless if you don't tie it into your theme and provide a lesson learned.

Let's imagine a preacher is going to tell a biblical story. The Bible is full of sparkling dialogue. It doesn't say, "Jesus went out and had a conversation with the crowd." No! It says, "Jesus went out and said…" That's a perfect example of sparkling dialogue. Let's just imagine you are telling the story of Jesus turning the loaves and fishes into a feast.

›› List all the characters who are part of the story.

›› Determine the point of the story.

›› Tell the story as sparkling dialogue.

›› Give your characters flesh-and blood personalities that your audience can relate to.

›› Make your stories come alive.

›› Good stories should be edited down to the nub and then acted out for greatest impact.

Learn to affect the role of that character on stage by shifting your position, changing your head movement or facial expression. In this way the audience can see the story and appreciate it more.

DM: I notice you use humor in your presentations. What are some guidelines for using humor?

PF: Humor can add a lot to your sermon, but it must fit you and your topic. Use humor with caution. Before you use humor, ask yourself these questions:

›› Is it appropriate to the occasion and for the audience?

›› Is it in good taste?

›› Does it support your topic or its key points?

Avoid telling generic "funny stories." Rather, find and build humor within the context of your own stories. Jokes may get a laugh, but a humorous personal story pertinent to your talk will add freshness and will be memorable to your audience.

DM: Many preachers receive little or no training in the area of nonverbal communication. What practical pointers can you share that would help preachers communicate effectively through body language?

PF: Body language is an essential part of your message and can help you enhance the words you use to create pictures in the minds of your audience. Move on purpose. Let your movement be phrase specific. If you are saying, "Moses came down from the mountaintop," or "Jesus returned from 40 days in the desert," those would be appropriate times to move.

Avoid repetitive use of the same movements or gestures. Practice a variety of movements. Try practicing a sermon by clasping your hands behind your back to avoid meaningless, repetitive arm and hand gestures. It will be tough at first to concentrate on your sermon without using your hands, but it will help stop superficial flailing and gesturing.

You can use movement for emphasis. To emphasize a shift in your sermon content, move to the left or right of the lectern. If you have a strong point to make, use that moment to take a step or two forward to emphasize that issue. When you are making that key point, stand still and deliver. After making a point or delivering a punch line, accentuate it by standing still and shifting only your eyes. The impact will be much greater.

Movement rehearsal is essential to ensure your gestures are relevant and not superficial or redundant. It is important not to overdo the same gestures or to stand inert before your audience. Movement keeps your presence fresh.

DM: What lessons have you learned as a professional speaker that have been most helpful for you?

PF: One of the most exciting elements of presentations I have learned is the art of not using my voice.

Pausing at exactly the right moment in your sermon is often more effective than anything you could do with your voice or body movements. Learn to pause more often. Knowing your material very well may cause you to talk too fast. Your audience may be hearing your information for the first time, so it is important to slow down and give them the opportunity to catch every word. Using pauses and silences to punctuate your material will draw in your audience.

I've also learned the importance of packaging and polishing.

When working on a new talk, develop the habit of reciting it to yourself repeatedly. You can do this while driving the car, walking through the park, waiting in an airport. After every statement or segment of material, ask yourself "Who cares?" If no one really does, don't say it.

Ask yourself, "Does this material dilute the message or enhance it?" "Does this material make the sermon more interesting, or does it make the sermon so long that the audience loses the point?" This is a great way to see if you are saying anything of value. Use short, simple declarative sentences and cut out useless words. Sound bites can be more effective than lengthy dissertations. Do this until the words form a harmonious pattern with which you are comfortable. Then dictate it on a recorder and have it transcribed on paper.

Now undertake the tightening, fine-tuning, polishing process. Check for grammatical errors, delete unnecessary words, highlight the punch words, and find the emotion you want behind the words.

Then run it by close friends or associates for their feedback. Keep an open mind to constructive criticism, continue to make refinements, add pauses or gestures to draw in the audience, and insert ideas from others that enhance the integrity of the material. Once you've completed this process, proceed to final rehearsals until it is second nature to you and you can relax with it in front of your audience.

Remember words are not enough. People always work on the words, but they seldom work on how they say them. Always look for ways to add pace, spice, energy, and polish. Try it! You will be amazed at how dynamic a sermon can become by doing your homework dutifully and taking the time to craft it into a polished piece of work.

~

CHAPTER 22 — REFLECTION/DISCUSSION QUESTIONS

1. How do you respond to Fripp's suggestions about dealing with nervousness prior to preaching a sermon? What techniques have you used in your preaching ministry to channel your nervous energy in a creative way?

2. Who has helped you develop your storytelling abilities? What lessons have you learned?

3. What suggestions regarding the delivery of a sermon do you plan to implement in your preaching ministry?

TWENTY-THREE
PREACHING EFFECTIVELY WITHOUT NOTES

W̲ould you like to move your preaching ministry to a higher level of effectiveness? Try preaching without notes.[1] Many preachers are convinced that finding freedom from their sermon notes will enable them to connect more effectively with their listeners.[2] The question is not "Why should I try preaching without notes?" but "How?"

What follows is a simple five-step process that will help you preach effectively without notes.

Step #1: Begin your sermon preparation early

Wise long-term preparation should include the development of a preaching calendar.[3] This advance preparation will help you avoid wasted time. At the beginning of each week, with your starting point clear and your preaching passage already selected, you'll want to make sure you schedule regular time for sermon preparation. Without a plan, the tyranny of the urgent will take over. We've all heard horror stories about preachers who prepare their sermons the night before their preaching appointment, or even later. Such lack of planning does not honor God or contribute to the physical, emotional, and spiritual health of the preacher. You'll want to begin your sermon preparation early so that doesn't happen to you. Carefully and prayerfully study your preaching passage and gather notes at the beginning of the week. Do not begin writing your sermon manuscript until you have identified your single dominant preaching idea, decided on a sermon form, and crafted your sermon outline.

Step #2: Write the first draft of your sermon manuscript

No later than three days prior to your preaching appointment, write the first draft of your sermon manuscript. Perhaps you thought preaching without notes would eliminate the need for a sermon manuscript. Not so.[4] Preaching without notes does not substitute for the discipline of writing, and it does not qualify as a shortcut. Rather, preaching without notes is a step beyond the written manuscript and necessitates the writing of the first draft of your sermon manuscript early in the week. Make sure you write an oral document.[5] Your sermon is not an essay or an article, but a creative and engaging conversation with your listeners. Vocalize the sermon while you write. According to William Shepherd, "it is when we actually hear words spoken that we notice the subtle differences between written and oral language."[6] So write aloud. Don't be concerned about writing a "perfect sermon" on the first draft. This is the beginning, not the end. Pray while you write the first draft of your sermon manuscript. The Holy Spirit wants to be with you just as much in the preparation as in the preaching. This early "birthing" of your sermon manuscript allows time for the next step, which is crucial in preparing to preach effectively without notes.

Step #3: Internalize your sermon

During the last two days of preparation, walk through your sermon like a tour guide becoming acquainted with this new attraction. Use your sermon manuscript like a map. Your goal is not rote memorization but internalization.[7] Walking through your sermon will test its structure[8] and highlight the need for additions or deletions to your sermon manuscript. Early in the internalization process, walking through your sermon will require your full and undivided attention.[9] Take notes. After each walkthrough, make revisions to your sermon manuscript. Later in the internalization process, you can walk through your sermon while engaged in other activities, such as taking a shower, driving to an appointment, or waiting in line. Walking through your sermon right before you go to bed very effectively lodges the sermon in your memory.[10]

This process of internalizing your sermon will also enable you to address issues of oral interpretation and nonverbal communication. The words themselves are just a small part of the communication process. How will you say those words, and what gestures and facial expressions will you use? Allow at least 25 percent of your total sermon preparation time to internalize your sermon.[11] This is a time of revision and rehearsal. By the end of this internalization process, you will be well acquainted with all the moves and submoves of your tour. Like a skilled tour guide, you are now prepared to lead your listeners over well-traveled territory.

Step #4: Do a last-minute walkthrough

Immediately prior to your preaching appointment, do a last-minute walkthrough of your sermon. Prayerfully review only the main moves of your sermon. This last-minute walkthrough should take sixty seconds or less. There is no need to panic. Do not concern yourself with all the details of your sermon. Most of those details will be recalled as you lead your listeners on the now familiar sermon tour. Don't be anxious about details that might be omitted. Joseph M. Webb emphasizes that "even though everything is well prepared, the preacher stands in front of people literally thinking out loud. The ideas have been worked through, both consciously and unconsciously; but even after the ideas have been outlined and memorized, they are refined and rethought right up to and even through the course of the sermon delivery."[12] This inductive speech mode increases a sense of anticipation and discovery both for the listeners and for the preacher. So don't be anxious. That which you lose by leaving your sermon manuscript behind is minor compared to that gained in effective communication. Conclude your last-minute preparation by reviewing the first few sentences of your sermon. Know exactly where you are going to begin when you stand up to preach. With a clear and compelling introduction, your listeners will fall in step alongside as you lead the tour.

Step #5: Listen while you preach

During the preaching of your sermon, ask the Lord to help you remember the important message and forget the unnecessary. Ask Him to help you be attentive to your listeners. Give Him permission to bring new insights to your attention that will be helpful as you lead the sermon tour. Freedom from your sermon notes will enable you to be much more attentive to the verbal and nonverbal responses of your listeners. Remember that all effective communication is dialogue. So listen as well as speak. Listen to verbal responses and respond to them. Don't just look at your listeners in order to "establish good eye contact." Be attentive to their nonverbal feedback. Like a skilled tour guide, repeat important points if it is evident you have not been heard. Pick up the pace of the tour or add an additional illustration if you sense that your listeners are losing interest. Your goal is not to repeat all the words of your sermon manuscript but rather to help your listeners receive maximum benefit from the tour.

Be prepared to experience a degree of awkwardness when you preach your first sermon without notes. That's normal. Don't panic or give up in despair. Recognize that any skill requires practice before it becomes a natural response. Do you remember when you learned to ride a bicycle without training wheels? It wasn't easy at first, was it? You felt unstable. Wobbly. Anxious. But with practice, you learned the skill. Before long, you could jump on your bicycle and enjoy your newfound freedom!

Preaching without notes requires practice too. So be patient with yourself. Allow yourself some time to develop the skill and listen to the feedback of your listeners.[13] I remember my first sermon without notes. After 20 years of preaching with a sermon manuscript, I had lost my training wheels, and I was stressed out! What if I lost my balance? What if I crashed? After first service, my wife gave me some helpful feedback by suggesting, "You're still acting like you have a sermon manuscript!" And she was right. I was confined behind the pulpit, desperately trying to retrieve all the words off my invisible document. Her counsel? "Just get up and preach!" I listened to her feedback, and my preaching experience second service was totally different. I felt free. Liberated. No more training wheels. Now I could focus on connecting with my listeners. That was many years ago, and I have never looked back!

I encourage you to give this five-step process a try.[14] If you have never preached without notes, or if you would like to preach more effectively without notes, this five-step process can help you on your journey. Take a deep breath. It's time to discard the training wheels. Preach without notes and move your preaching ministry to a higher level of effectiveness.

~

CHAPTER 23 — REFLECTION/DISCUSSION QUESTIONS

1. How do you respond to the idea of preaching without notes? What thoughts and feelings come to mind when you imagine yourself preaching without notes?

2. Who has modeled for you the art of preaching effectively without notes?

3. What insights in this chapter are most helpful for you as you prepare to preach without notes?

Notes:

1. "Preaching Effectively Without Notes." *Ministry* October 2006. Reprinted by permission.

1. Charles W. Koller, in his classic work *Expository Preaching Without Notes,* recognizes that certain preachers preach effectively from a manuscript or sermon notes, but "the same preachers would be even more effective if they could stand note free in the pulpit" (Grand Rapids, MI: Baker Book House,1962), 34. This classic volume has been combined with Koller's book *Sermons Preached Without Notes* and has been reprinted as *How To Preach Without Notes* (Grand Rapids, MI: Baker Books, 1997).

2. Joseph M. Webb, in his excellent book *Preaching Without Notes,* suggests that preaching without notes will also maximize audience participation and reflect an authentic witness who speaks from the heart (Nashville, TN: Abingdon Press, 2001), 25–30.

3. For help in developing a preaching calendar, see chapter 25.

4. I disagree with Webb on this crucial step. I consider the writing of an oral manuscript an essential part of preparing to preach without notes.

5. For a helpful presentation on writing an oral manuscript, see William H. Shepherd's book *Without a Net: Preaching in a Paperless Pulpit* (Lima, OH: CSS Publishing Company 2004), 100–121.

6. Shepherd, Without a Net, 103.

7. Shepherd notes that "we learn our sermons as actors learn their lines, but unlike most actors, we have the freedom to improve our lines as we rehearse, and even as we deliver the sermon." Without a Net, 123.

8. A clear and logical outline is of the utmost importance when preparing to preach a sermon without notes.

9. This initial walk-through of your sermon is best performed overtly, out loud. Later in the internalization process, the walk-through can be covert, in your head.

10. That is, assuming that you are not physically or mentally exhausted. Good physical and mental health is essential for optimal memory function.

11. A common error in sermon preparation is leaving inadequate time for internalization. As a result, preachers are all too often preoccupied with words when they preach rather than focusing on connecting with their listeners. I would recommend walking through your sermon four to six times during this internalization process.

12. *Preaching Without Notes,* 28.

13. Shepherd suggests that a preacher just learning to preach without notes might "pick a small section of the sermon and resolve to preach that section—and only that section—without referring to your manuscript. Pick a story first, since stories are easily remembered. Preach your sermon as before, but when it comes time for the story, look up at your audience and keep your eyes there. Let the story come. Next week, pick another part of the sermon....Gradually build up your confidence so that you can do two or three thought units each week without referring to your manuscript." *Without a Net,* 133.

14. Your experiences as you experiment with this five-step process for preaching effectively without notes will be helpful to other preachers. Send feedback, comments, or suggestions to dmorris@powerfulbiblcalpreaching.com.

TWENTY-FOUR
FEEDBACK AND EVALUATION

Lee Strobel, once a spiritual skeptic, worked as an award-winning journalist for thirteen years with the Chicago Tribune and other newspapers. Since becoming a Christian, Strobel has served as a teaching pastor at two of the largest Christian churches in the world—Willow Creek Community Church and Saddleback Community Church.

DEREK MORRIS (DM): Lee, you have served as a teaching pastor at two of the largest Christian churches in the world.[1] Prior to joining the staff at Saddleback Community Church, you served as a teaching pastor at Willow Creek Community Church. Both churches have a strong commitment to relevant biblical preaching. You have mentioned that feedback and evaluation have been key factors in your growth and development as a communicator of relevant biblical messages. Please explain.

LEE STROBEL (LS): For me, pre-delivery evaluation is really important. I don't think I have ever spoken without getting some pre-sermon feedback. I finish a preliminary draft of my sermon manuscript by Thursday night. On Friday morning I'll give it to at least one person. He critiques it and I expect him to be honest. Sometimes he scrawls at the end, "This is tremendous! God is going to use this." Other times he recommends I make this or that change. A lot of times he will make suggestions, such as "I think this passage of Scripture would really be meaningful at this juncture." After a written critique of the sermon is completed, we have lunch together and discuss it. I take his advice about 80 percent of the time. I feel free to say, "I disagree. Thanks for the input, but I don't agree with that."

DM: What then?

LS: I don't do much work on the sermon Friday afternoon, but then something happens that I call "the Friday night miracle." That is when the Holy Spirit helps me put the final touch on the message.

DM: Bill Hybels mentioned that if he has a question or concern about something in his sermon, he might also solicit some pre-sermon feedback before he preaches the sermon for the first time.

LS: Yes. If we are addressing a really sensitive issue on which the church doesn't have a clearly defined position, we might solicit pre-sermon feedback from the elders. For instance, a couple years ago, when I preached a series on evolution and creation, I got some pre-sermon feedback from one of the elders and from Bill.

DM: Having preached a sermon for the first time, as you usually do on a Saturday night, do you always receive post-sermon feedback in preparation for presenting the sermon again during Sunday services?

LS: Yes. We all receive post-sermon feedback, though it varies considerably. Sometimes it is written; other times it is verbal. On one occasion I received a six-minute voice mail message to which I responded from my car as I was driving home.

DM: One of the things Bill Hybels emphasizes is that when soliciting feedback and evaluation for your sermons, you have to ask the right people the right questions at the right time. It is unwise to invite people at random to provide feedback, because you get distortion. Some people are trying to impress you; some people have an ax to grind. How many individuals provide you with post-sermon feedback?

LS: There are three individuals who provide me with post-sermon feedback. I would be suspicious if someone enthusiastically volunteered to critique my messages. I would wonder why.

DM: How does post-sermon feedback on Saturday evening impact your preaching at the Sunday services?

LS: It could be a word, a movement, a gesture. Once somebody noticed that when I made a point I would step backward from the podium instead of stepping forward, which is more powerful. That was great feedback! Another person said, "You are scanning the people, but you are not focusing." I would say 80 percent of the time there is at least one suggestion for fine-tuning the sermon. The feedback, however, is not always a suggestion. Sometimes it is simply an affirmation. One of the elders likes to write "Waverly Avenue!" That means "home run!" because when a home run is hit at Wrigley Field, home of the Chicago Cubs, it goes out onto Waverly Avenue.

DM: Do you always implement the suggestions you receive?

LS: No. It's important for speakers to have the freedom to disagree and do what they think is right in the end. I listen carefully to all the feedback, and I disagree with about 30 percent of it. Sometimes the suggestion is too radical. It is too late on Saturday evening to tell me to implement a totally different structure for the sermon. That's a suggestion that cannot be implemented by Sunday morning. Rather, I need to know how I can work with what I have to make it better.

DM: Do you receive any post-sermon feedback after the Sunday services?

LS: The senior pastor, Bill Hybels, always gets a sermon tape and offers some feedback. If he is out of town, I may receive the feedback several days later, but it provides additional helpful advice and input that I can implement in the future.

DM: As you look back and consider how feedback and evaluation have helped you to preach relevant biblical sermons, could you imagine ceasing any feedback at this point and just going on without it?

LS: I wouldn't want to. That is why I solicit feedback before the message. I want the feedback because I know this is the only way I am going to grow. If you are in an environment where for some reason the people feel the speaker's ego is too fragile, or he or she is too insecure, or there is something wrong with the community that people feel reluctant to provide feedback, it doesn't mean they don't still have opinions. I want to know what my listeners are thinking. I want them to feel free to be able to communicate with me so I can improve.

DM: If evaluation and feedback are such valuable resources for preaching relevant biblical sermons, why do you think so few preachers solicit feedback and evaluation of their sermons?

LS: Some preachers may not enjoy a level of community where there is trust, love, and a feeling of security. It is not always pleasant to receive feedback. I wouldn't like being involved in an atmosphere where there is a lot of feedback and evaluation without a sense of community. I can remember one time I did a message on a Saturday evening and blew it big-time. There was just something wrong with the message, and I didn't know what. Bill pulled me aside and talked with me for about two hours after that message. Now, this was very early in my preaching. It was probably the fifth message I had ever given in my life. I stayed up all night and worked on the message, then gave it two more reviews the next day, and it was much better. But if I had not been in community with Bill, if I had not known that Bill really loved and valued me, that would have been a very devastating encounter. So I think evaluation and feedback have to be in the context of community.

Just recently I did a Scripture slide service and felt very good about it. However, the feedback I immediately got after the Saturday evening meeting was that I needed to cut a section of it that I really liked. As I thought about it, I realized that I enjoyed this section because of the response I received, but it didn't really contribute to what we were trying to accomplish in the service. At first, receiving such feedback can be a blow to your self-esteem, and it can sting, but the sting goes away very quickly when the salve of the whole community is applied.

DM: I hear you saying that a loving, caring community is an essential context for feedback and evaluation. If that sense of community is missing, it's easy for a preacher to become defensive. Can you think of any other reasons preachers might resist feedback and evaluation of their sermons?

LS: I wonder if some preachers have the feeling they are a cut above everyone else. They may be the dominant, autocratic type who believe no one should dare to question what they do or evaluate what they say. They might feel free to evaluate everybody else, but have great difficulty with anybody assessing them. To me, such an attitude is a community killer. Bill Hybels not only accepts the evaluation and feedback of his sermons, he solicits it. Some pastors feel if they allow themselves to be vulnerable enough to be critiqued, it somehow diminishes their leadership or impairs their status. They think such input somehow knocks them down a notch. But I don't think so.

DM: Lee, it has been exciting to hear from someone who has a real passion for relevant biblical preaching. Thank you for the practical suggestions you have shared with us that can help us connect effectively with our listeners and preach relevant biblical sermons.

~

CHAPTER 24 — REFLECTION/DISCUSSION QUESTIONS

1. How do you feel about receiving sermon feedback? What are some of the benefits and dangers associated with feedback and evaluation?

2. What are some ways that you solicit feedback from your listeners?

3. What are some practical ways that you can build community so that feedback and evaluation can be given in a safe and loving context?

Notes:

1. "Feedback and Evaluation." An interview with Lee Strobel, *Ministry* January 2001. Reprinted by permission.

TWENTY-FIVE
PLANNING YOUR PREACHING CALENDAR

I still remember my panic as a young preacher.[1] With the early part of each week slipping through my fingers like dry sand, I would be staring at a bulletin deadline: the time my sermon title was due. That meant I had a sermon to write, but didn't even know where to begin.

I can remember browsing through religious periodicals, desperately searching for inspiration. At times, I found myself giving the church secretary a generic sermon title like "The Love of God," hoping for enlightenment later in the week!

How can a preacher avoid this weekly panic attack? Here is one practical suggestion: plan an annual preaching calendar. Most ministers will admit there are benefits to a preaching calendar, but many don't know where to begin. Here's a simple process (tested in the local church) for developing such an annual calendar.

Step #1: Select a Sermon Planning Group

Personally select a group of 12-15 members from your congregation to serve on a Sermon Planning Group. Look for individuals representative of the diversity of your congregation (age, gender, ethnicity, and religious heritage). Give this Sermon Planning Group a 30-day assignment. Ask each member to solicit feedback from family members, neighbors, and friends about topics that would interest them in the coming year. Encourage group members to develop specific recommendations of sermon series that would connect with the individuals they have contacted. You will be surprised how seriously individuals take hold of this assignment!

Begin this process four months prior to the beginning of your preaching calendar. This allows adequate time to work through the process and still provide some lead time for the worship teams to plan services at the beginning of the preaching calendar.

It is helpful to change the composition of the Sermon Planning Group annually. This provides opportunity for a broad cross-section of the congregation to participate. It also avoids the criticism that a handful of members are controlling the preaching calendar of the church.

Step #2: Schedule a reporting session

Bring your Sermon Planning Group together for a reporting session. Take notes. Writing suggestions on a whiteboard or large notepad helps group members see emerging patterns.

Several individuals may suggest a series of sermons on a similar theme, or on a particular book of the Bible. Decide together the best format and length for each series. Solicit group feedback regarding titles.[2] By the end of this reporting session, you should have a collection of sermon series.

Allow a minimum of four hours for this reporting session. You may decide to take the Sermon Planning Group to a retreat center for the day or even for a weekend. Either way, if you spend a minimum of a full day with your Sermon Planning Group, you should be able to complete a rough draft of your preaching calendar. Adequate time spent doing step #2 will save time later in the process.

Step #3: Solicit feedback from leadership team

Solicit feedback from other pastors on your staff or from key lay leaders. While these individuals may not have participated directly in the group work mentioned above, they are sensitive to the needs of the church family.

Give them an opportunity to review the rough draft of the calendar. Encourage them to make suggestions, either adding to, deleting, or modifying the recommendations of the Sermon Planning Group. During this third step, you may also determine who will be responsible for each preaching assignment.

Step #4: Reflect, revise and refine

Step four is a time for you to prayerfully reflect on your proposed preaching assignments. Take the revised draft of the preaching calendar with you, along with any notes from the reporting session. Consider the flow from one sermon series to another.

As you look at the bigger picture, you will begin to see what needs have not been addressed. Make additions, deletions, and modifications, fitting into any liturgical or denominational plans you may need to observe. Then, make a calendar and assign a specific weekend for each sermon.

As part of the preaching calendar, include a proposed sermon title, preaching passage, and preaching idea.

The benefits

Planning a preaching calendar takes time, but the benefits far exceed the cost.

First, as mentioned, having a preaching calendar helps you avoid the weekly panic attack that comes from last-minute sermon preparation. Beginning the sermon preparation process weeks or even months ahead provides incubation time for you to process ideas.

Once your preaching calendar is complete, you can create a file for each sermon. As you find relevant resources or ideas, drop them into the appropriate file. Then, as you begin your sermon preparation, you will not only know your basic direction, but you will also have resources to work with.

Second, a carefully planned preaching calendar helps to ensure balance in the spiritual diet of your congregation. The apostle Paul reminded the Ephesian elders that, during his extended time of ministry in Ephesus, he had declared to them "the whole counsel of God" (Acts 20:27).

A balanced preaching calendar will include both the Old Testament and the New Testament, and will cover the broad themes of the Bible as well as issues of practical concern for everyday Christian living.

The one-sermon pastor who preaches the same sermon every week with a few minor variations bores the congregation and leaves them spiritually malnourished. A lack of prayerful, intentional planning can also result in myopic preaching preoccupied with chasing after immediate concerns while failing to declare the whole counsel of God.

Third, a preaching calendar also enables your worship teams to plan ahead. You may not actually begin to write a specific sermon until the first part of the week, but the worship team assigned to that weekend can plan weeks or even months ahead, designing a worship service around your preaching passage and preaching idea. Even though your preaching idea may be modified, the basic theme will remain the same.

Fourth, with advance notice regarding upcoming sermons, your communications team can provide articles for local newspapers and make postings on your church Web site. You can also encourage church members to plan ahead and invite family members, neighbors, and friends to an upcoming sermon series.

There will inevitably be a few times during the year when your preaching calendar will need to be modified. Events of regional or global significance cannot be ignored. Unexpected transitions in the congregation might also necessitate the addition of a sermon not originally scheduled. At times like these, make prayerful adjustments to your preaching calendar. Such changes create a certain amount of disequilibrium, but they are the exception rather than the rule.

If you are experiencing weekly panic attacks as a result of last-minute sermon preparation, try planning a preaching calendar. It's a valuable tool which will help you to move from panic to purpose in your preaching.

~

CHAPTER 25 — REFLECTION/DISCUSSION QUESTIONS

1. Reflect on times when you felt stressed due to rushed sermon preparation. Which of those times were unavoidable and which could have been prevented by careful planning?

2. How do you currently plan your preaching schedule?

3. Which suggestions from this chapter will you implement in order to move toward a more purposeful preaching ministry?

Notes:

1. "From Panic to Purpose: The Process and Benefits of Planning a Preaching Calendar." *Ministry* September 2004. Reprinted by permission.

2. One of my Sermon Planning Groups showed a tremendous amount of creativity. They sensed the need for sermons that connect with everyday life. One four-part series that they suggested was entitled "Christianity in the Marketplace." This sermon series included "Being Christian in the Classroom," "Being Christian in the Care-Giving Professions," "Being Christian in Business," and "Being Christian at Home." For more information on this series, see Chapter 21. Sermon manuscripts for this series are available at www.powerfulbiblical-preaching.com.

TWENTY-SIX
HOW TO CARE FOR YOUR VOICE

just signed up for voice lessons.[1] No, I am not planning to stop preaching and become a professional singer! Rather, I want to learn how to care for my voice in order to maximize and preserve my impact as a preacher for years to come. Most of us received little or no instruction in voice care during our college or seminary training. Many of our preaching professors assumed we all knew how to take care of our voices. They were wrong. That is why I have dialogued with several voice professionals in order to discover some practical suggestions about voice care for preachers.[2]

Your voice is a miracle of creative genius. Your vocal cords are quite small, somewhere between 18–23 millimeters in size, and this miraculous and priceless instrument is housed within your larynx. Your vocal cords vibrate hundreds of times per second when speaking. Continuous misuse or abuse will damage them, and sometimes that damage becomes permanent.

If you would like to protect and preserve your vocal cords and keep your voice working at peak performance, here are eight practical suggestions for voice care:

1. Warm up your vocal cords

Athletes use a warm-up routine before vigorous exercise. This reduces the risk of injury to muscles and ensures peak performance. Likewise, your vocal cords are muscles, too, and they need to be "warmed up" before use in order to realize their maximum potential and avoid injury.

A simple warm-up exercise for speakers involves humming on a descending scale. Your lips should be touching, with your teeth slightly separated. Feel the buzzing sensation when humming. You can also vocalize various syllables on a descending scale. Try using buzzing sounds like vi, vi, vi, vi, vi; va, va, va, va, va; vo, vo, vo, vo, vo; or bede, bede, bede, bede, bede; or ze, za, zo, zu. Start in the middle of your range and descend to your low range. Then go to your high range and descend to your middle range. You can also do lip trills (make a brrr sound, vibrating your lips naturally and easily). A few minutes devoted to a vocal warm-up routine is time well spent.

Gale Jones Murphy, a renowned Christian musician and motivational speaker, offers this practical suggestion for a vocal warm-up routine for preachers. Before a busy day of preaching, one of the best times and locations to warm up your voice is while taking a shower. The steam and humidity are great for the vocal cords. Sing the melodies of some of your favorite hymns or Scripture songs with ee vowels, remembering to relax your jaw. This focused warm-up routine can also be a time of spiritual reflection as you associate the melodies with the spiritual messages of the songs.[3]

If you find yourself running out of breath in just a few seconds during your warm-up exercises, then you need to pay special attention to the second suggestion below.

2. Practice proper breathing techniques

The vibration of your vocal cords requires consistent, continuous airflow—this reinforces why proper breathing techniques are essential for peak vocal performance. Be mindful of proper breath management because too much pressure wears down the vocal cords. However, too little pressure has the same negative effect. Here are several breathing exercises to help you develop effective breath support:

» Inhale deeply, allowing your ribcage to expand and your diaphragm to lower without raising your shoulders. Then exhale slowly with a hissing sound, gently pulling in with your abdominal muscles for a consistent airflow through your vocal cords. Think about sucking through a clogged straw while inhaling. This will help your air intake to flow slowly and smoothly.

» Inhale deeply, then vocalize "Choo, choo, choo" with a loud whisper, using your abdominal muscles to pull in and up with each word. Learn to associate the use of your voice with good breathing techniques. These breathing exercises also help minimize upper body and neck tension and fatigue.

›› Lie on the floor with a large book on your abdomen and breathe. The book should ascend and descend as you inhale and exhale. You can also practice this breathing exercise while lying in bed.

›› Explore the extremes between too much air pressure and too little air pressure. Exhale with a loud hissing sound (too much air pressure). Then exhale with no hissing sound (too little air pressure). Develop muscle memory for an appropriate breath support that produces better tone quality. Practice reciting sermons with passion without developing tension in your throat.

›› Learn to breathe deeply. Engage in activities such as brisk walking, biking, and other aerobic exercises that require you to breathe deeply. Panting can also help you to breathe deeply. Start slowly, then speed up. Feel your whole torso moving when you pant, not just your chest. Deep breathing gets the diaphragm to lower, which produces a more efficient and pleasing tone. Intentionally wake up your body by deep breathing prior to a speaking appointment.

3. Practice good posture

Good posture is essential for efficient voice production. When your physical alignment is poor, you not only look awkward to your congregation, but you also impair proper breathing techniques. Have you noticed preachers who slump over the pulpit? That is an example of poor posture. When you have proper body alignment, you should be able to drop a line from the top of your head, past your ear, the point of your shoulder, the highest point of your pelvis, just behind your kneecap, and just in front of your ankle. Proper posture enables you to have good balance, move freely, and provide efficient breath support.

4. Provide adequate hydration

My colleague, Dr. Evan Chesney, often coaches me in good voice care with a single word: "Hydrate!"[4] Most of us are aware that our bodies are made up of approximately 60 percent water. Lost water needs to be replaced daily, and the best way to hydrate is to drink pure water. Other fluids, like juices, are not good substitutes for pure water because your body processes these fluids as food and treats them differently.[5]

Adequate hydration with pure water becomes particularly important for the lubrication of your vocal cords. Make sure you are well hydrated before speaking and, if necessary, drink additional water during breaks. Room temperature water is preferable because chilled water will cause the vocal cords to constrict. When preaching multiple times in one day, I make sure I drink at least 16 ounces (0.47 liters) of water prior to my first sermon and an additional 16 ounces of water between each sermon. I thought I was doing well until Reyna Carguill shared with me that she drinks 64–128 ounces (1.89–3.79 liters) of water in the four hours preceding a major event.[6] This requires some intentionality, but adequate hydration is well worth the effort in order to avoid damage to inadequately hydrated vocal cords.

Mark Becker shared a story with me that illustrates the importance of adequate hydration.[7] A preacher requested Becker's assistance because he noticed that his throat was beginning to get sore during his speaking assignments. In asking for help, the preacher demonstrated wisdom because soreness is your body's way of telling you something is wrong, and you could be damaging some aspect of your physical being. After careful analysis, it was discovered that the preacher was sipping water during his sermons. Rather than providing adequate hydration, this sipping habit was simply washing away the natural lubrication from around his vocal cords, resulting in soreness. When the preacher began to drink adequate fluids prior to speaking and on breaks, rather than sipping water during his presentations, he was able to speak all day without soreness of any kind.

5. Get adequate rest

Has anyone ever said to you, "You sound tired!" When you are tired, one of the first parts of your body to be affected is your voice. Adequate rest is essential for optimal voice performance. Reyna Carguill makes a point of getting extra rest two days before a major event. Preachers also need to give their bodies some rest reserves. Be intentional as well about providing rest for your vocal cords. Have you heard the expression "Silence is golden"? That is true, not only in times of conflict, but also when you want to provide good care for your voice. Vocal rest becomes very beneficial for your instrument. Be silent for an extended period of time. Some preachers have the mistaken idea that whispering rests the vocal cords, but nothing could be further from the truth. In fact, whispering is more stressful on your vocal cords than speaking. So take time to just be silent. Rest.

If you have a demanding speaking schedule on a particular day, schedule time for your vocal cords to rest. Ask someone else to welcome the visitors, give the announcements, lead the songs, and offer the morning prayer. Make room for others to serve, while providing rest periods for your voice at the same time.

6. Provide healthy fuel for your body

Your whole body supports your voice so make sure you provide your body with healthy fuel. Everything you eat and drink either sustains or alters your nutritional balance. To maintain the proper chemical balance in your body, you need the appropriate nutrients. Enjoy a healthy balance of fruits, vegetables, grains, nuts, and legumes. Be aware of foods and beverages that can damage your instrument; for example, spicy foods and fried foods can cause acid reflux that damage the vocal cords. Also, be aware of personal food allergies that can affect vocal performance. Avoid overeating which results in shallow breathing and lack of energy. Adequate and appropriate nutrition prior to speaking helps provide the needed energy for peak performance.[8]

7. Keep your whole body toned

Exercise is also essential for optimal vocal performance, for exercise will keep your body toned and enhance your core strength. Many muscles are engaged when speaking, and a well-toned muscular system will help you maximize your impact as a communicator. Dr. Julie Penner strongly encourages all her voice students to take an exercise class that concentrates on strengthening the core of the body, namely the innermost abdominals.[9] This exercise class also involves stretching and controlled deep breathing, all of which results in freedom and support of the voice and helps the speaker or singer become more supple in body and voice.

8. Take some voice lessons

Every preacher could benefit from taking some voice lessons from a good vocal coach. Dr. Evan Chesney shared a lesson he learned early in his career: "My first teaching experience began when I taught remedial English at Southern Adventist University. After my first week of teaching, I had pretty much trashed my voice, which was very frustrating since I was a vocal performance major. My voice teacher pointed out that I needed to learn to speak the same way I sing. Applying the same techniques when speaking that I used in singing—proper posture, abdominal breath support, proper vocal placement and projection—relieved the stress on my vocal cords, and I didn't have any more trouble."

Your voice teacher can help you avoid voice strain and provide some helpful strategies to protect your precious instrument.[10] Old habits die hard, but it is possible to change with discipline and practice. If you are experiencing a vocal disorder of some kind, your voice teacher might suggest you consult a physician because your vocal cords could be damaged and may require complete rest or even surgery.

Your voice is a precious gift. Do not misuse or abuse it. Make an effort to practice good voice care. Be determined to use your voice to bring honor and glory to God.[11]

~

CHAPTER 26 — REFLECTION/DISCUSSION QUESTIONS

1. Think of an occasion when your voice was affected either by sickness or poor voice care. What were your thoughts and feelings during that time?

2. Which of the eight practical suggestions for voice care listed in this chapter are you currently following in order to protect and preserve your voice?

3. What new insight have you gained from this chapter that will enhance your voice care?

Notes:

1. "How to Care for Your Voice." *Ministry* July/August 2010. Reprinted by permission.
2. I am grateful to Mark Becker, Reyna Carguill, Dr. Evan Chesney, Gale Jones Murphy, and Dr. Julie Penner for their significant contributions to this article.
3. Gale Jones Murphy serves as a choral teacher at Brentwood Academy in Brentwood, Tennessee.
4. Dr. Evan Chesney serves as the minister of music at the Forest Lake Seventh-day Adventist Church in Apopka, Florida.
5. Alcohol and caffeinated drinks are also detrimental to optimal vocal performance. Alcohol causes constriction of the blood vessels in the vocal cords, causing a reduction in vocal control. Caffeine causes dryness in the throat and impairs a healthy rest cycle.
6. Reyna Carguill is a professional operatic soprano.
7. Mark Becker teaches voice lessons and directs choral and handbell activities at Forest Lake Academy in Apopka, Florida.
8. A healthy lifestyle is an important part of caring for your voice. An excellent resource for whole person health is CREATION Health, which is produced by Florida Hospital. You can learn more about CREATION Health at www.creationhealth.tv.
9. Dr. Julie Penner is the director of voice activities at Southern Adventist University in Collegedale, Tennessee.
10. Preachers need to learn how to use a microphone correctly. You should not adjust your speaking voice in an attempt to find the appropriate volume or tone. That is the job of the audio technician. Take time for an audio check. The equalizer levels (EQ) are different for speaking versus singing. Female voices may require less treble and male voices may require less bass tones.
11. An excellent user-friendly book on the use and care of the voice is *The Performer's Voice* by Meribeth Bunch Dayme (New York, NY: W. W. Norton, 2005). For a more technical book on vocal pedagogy, Dr. Julie Penner recommends *Your Voice: An Inside View by Scott McCoy* (Princeton, NJ: Inside View Press, 2006). A helpful Web site on voice care is www.your-personal-singing-guide.com.

BIBLIOGRAPHY

Akin, Daniel L., David L. Allen and Ned L. Matthews, eds. *Text-Driven Preaching: God's Word at the Heart of Every Sermon.* Nashville, TN: B & H Academic, 2010.

Arthurs, Jeffrey D. *Preaching with Variety: How to Recreate the Dynamic of Biblical Genres.* Grand Rapids, MI: Kregel, 2007.

Begg, Alistair. *Preaching for God's Glory.* Wheaton, IL: Crossway Books, 1999.

Braga, James. *How to Prepare Bible Messages.* Revised ed. Sisters, OR: Multnomah Publishers, 2005.

Brown, Teresa L. Fry. *Delivering the Sermon: Voice, Body, and Animation in Proclamation.* Minneapolis, MN: Fortress Press, 2008.

Buttrick, David G. *Preaching Jesus Christ.* Philadelphia, PA: Fortress Press, 1988.

Carrick, John. *The Imperative of Preaching: A Theology of Sacred Rhetoric.* Edinburgh: Banner of Truth Trust, 2002.

Chapell, Bryan. *Christ-Centered Preaching: Redeeming the Expository Sermon.* 2nd ed. Grand Rapids, MI: Baker Academic, 2005.

___. *Using Illustrations to Preach with Power.* Grand Rapids, MI: Zondervan Publishing House, 1992.

Craddock, Fred B. *Preaching.* Nashville, TN: Abingdon, 1985.

Duduit, Michael, ed. *Handbook of Contemporary Preaching.* Nashville, TN: Broadman Press, 1992.

Edwards, J. Kent. *Deep Preaching: Creating Sermons That Go Beyond the Superficial.* Nashville, TN: B & H Academic, 2009.

____. *Effective First-Person Biblical Preaching.* Grand Rapids, MI: Zondervan, 2005.

Fasol, Al. *A Complete Guide to Sermon Delivery.* Nashville, TN: Broadman and Holman Publishers, 1996.

Freeman, Harold. *Variety in Biblical Preaching: Innovative Techniques and Fresh Forms.* Waco, TX: Word Books, 1987.

Galli, Mark and Craig Brian Larson. *Preaching That Connects: Using the Techniques of Journalists to Add Impact to Your Sermons.* Grand Rapids, MI: Zondervan, 1994.

Hamilton, Donald L. *Preaching With Balance: Achieving and Maintaining Biblical Priorities in Preaching.* Fearn, Scotland: Christian Focus Publications, 2007.

Hybels, Bill, Stuart Briscoe and Haddon Robinson. *Mastering Contemporary Preaching.* Portland, OR: Multnomah Press, 1989.

Johnson, Darrel W. *The Glory of Preaching: Participating in God's Transformation of the World.* Downers Grove, IL: InterVarsity Press, 2009.

Johnson, Dennis E. *Him We Proclaim: Preaching Christ from All the Scriptures.* Phillipsburg, NJ: P & R Publishing Company, 2007.

Johnson, Ronald W. *How Will They Hear If We Don't Listen: The Vital Role of Listening in Preaching and Personal Evangelism.* Nashville, TN: Broadman and Holman Publishers, 1994.

Kinlaw, Dennis F. *Preaching in the Spirit.* Grand Rapids, MI: Francis Asbury Press, 1985.

Larson, Craig Brian, ed. *Prophetic Preaching.* Peabody, MA: Henderson Publishers, 2012.

Lawson, Steven J. *Famine in the Land: A Passionate Call for Expository Preaching.* Chicago, IL: Moody Publishers, 2003.

Lewis, Ralph L. with Gregg Lewis. *Inductive Preaching: Helping People Listen.* Westchester, IL: Crossway Books, 1983.

Long, Thomas. *The Witness Of Preaching.* Louisville, KY: The Westminster Press, 1989.

Lowry, Eugene L. *How to Preach a Parable: Designs for Narrative Sermons.* Nashville, TN: Abingdon Press, 1989.

___. *The Homiletical Plot: The Sermon as Narrative Art Form.* Atlanta, GA: John Knox Press, 1980.

Lybrand, Fred R. *Preaching on Your Feet: Connecting God and the Audience in the Preaching Moment.* Nashville, TN: B & H Academic, 2008.

McDill, Wayne. *12 Essential Skills for Great Preaching.* Expanded 2nd ed. Nashville, TN: B & H Publishing Group, 2006.

Miller, Calvin. *Marketplace Preaching: How to Return the Sermon to Where it Belongs.* Grand Rapids, MI: Baker Books, 1995.

___. *The Empowered Communicator: 7 Keys to Unlocking an Audience.* Nashville, TN: Broadman and Holman Publishers, 1994.

Mitchell, Henry H. *Black Preaching: The Recovery of a Powerful Art.* Nashville, TN: Abingdon Press, 1990.

___. *Celebration and Experience in Preaching.* Nashville, TN: Abingdon Press, 1990.

Olford, Stephen F. and David L. Olford. *Anointed Expository Preaching.* Nashville, TN: B & H Publishing Group, 2003.

Robinson, Haddon W. *Biblical Preaching: The Development and Delivery of Expository Messages.* 2nd ed. Grand Rapids, MI: Baker Academic, 2001.

___. *Biblical Sermons: How Twelve Preachers Apply the Principles of Biblical Preaching.* Grand Rapids, MI: Baker Book House, 1989.

___. *Making a Difference in Preaching.* Grand Rapids, MI: Baker Books, 1999.

Robinson, Haddon W. and Craig Brian Larson, eds. *The Art and Craft of Biblical Preaching: A Comprehensive Resource for Today's Communicators.* Grand Rapids, MI: Zondervan, 2005.

Robinson, Haddon W. and Torrey W. Robinson. *It's All In How You Tell It: Preaching First-Person Expository Messages.* Grand Rapids, MI: Baker Books, 2003.

Shepherd, William H. Jr. *Without a Net: Preaching in the Paperless Pulpit.* Lima, OH: CSS Publishing Co., 2004.

Smith, Steven W. *Dying to Preach: Embracing the Cross in the Pulpit.* Grand Rapids, MI: Kregel, 2009.

Sunnukjian, Donald R. *Invitation to Biblical Preaching: Proclaiming Truth with Clarity and Relevance.* Grand Rapids, MI: Kregel, 2007.

Stanley, Andy and Lane Jones. *Communicating for a Change: Seven Keys to Irresistible Communication.* Sisters, OR: Multnomah Publishers, 2006.

Stott, John R. W. *Between Two Worlds: The Art of Preaching in the Twentieth Century.* Grand Rapids, MI: William B. Eerdmans, 1982.

Taylor, Gardner C. *How Shall They Preach?* Elgin, IL.: Progressive Baptist Publishing House, 1977.

Tilsdale, Leonora Tubbs. *Prophetic Preaching: A Pastoral Approach.* Louisville, KY: Westminster John Knox Press, 2010.

Webb, Joseph M. *Preaching Without Notes.* Nashville, TN: Abingdon Press, 2001.

Wiersbe, Warren W. *Preaching and Teaching with Imagination: The Quest for Biblical Ministry.* Wheaton, IL: Victor Books, 1994.

Willimon, William H. and Richard Lischer, eds. *The Concise Encyclopedia of Preaching.* Louisville, KY: John Knox/Westminster Press, 1995.

Wilson, Paul Scott. *The Four Pages of the Sermon: A Guide to Biblical Preaching.* Nashville, TN: Abingdon, 1999.

Wogaman, J Philip. *Speaking the Truth in Love: Prophetic preaching to a broken world.* Louisville, KY: Westminister John Knox Press, 1998.

Zacharias, Ravi. *Can Man Live Without God?* Dallas, TX: Word Publishing, 1994.

~

NOTES